Bittersweet

Bittersweet

Lessons from My Mother's Kitchen

MATT McALLESTER

[signature] August 15 2010

BLOOMSBURY

LONDON · BERLIN · NEW YORK

First published in Great Britain 2010

Copyright © 2010 by Matt McAllester

All the photographs are from the McAllester family's collection

The moral right of the author has been asserted

Bloomsbury Publishing, London, Berlin and New York

36 Soho Square, London W1D 3QY

A CIP catalogue record for this book is available from the British Library

ISBN 978 1 4088 0094 2
10 9 8 7 6 5 4 3 2 1

Typeset by Hewer Text UK Ltd, Edinburgh

Printed in Great Britain by Clays Ltd, St Ives plc

Mixed Sources
Product group from well-managed
forests and other controlled sources
www.fsc.org Cert no. SGS-COC-2061
© 1996 Forest Stewardship Council
FSC

www.bloomsbury.com/mattmcallester

For Pernilla

Matt and Jane on the pavement of Oxford Terrace in Edinburgh

1

My mother sat in her armchair by the window and asked me if I thought I was a good cook.

'Yeah,' I said. 'Not bad.'

'Do you always leave the book open?'

'Yes,' I said.

'Then you can't cook.' She laughed, but she wasn't joking. 'If you need to keep the book open, you're not really cooking.'

We had had this conversation before. It had a companion piece that went like this:

'Have you read Elizabeth David yet?'

'No, Mum.'

'If you want to know how to cook, read Elizabeth David. She'll tell you everything. Read *French Provincial Cooking*. Her books are marvellous. We all learned to cook from Elizabeth David.'

This conversation I had with my mother was our shared doorway into talking about food. There was so little we could share, so few topics I could introduce without risking her anger and delusions – my father, certain former friends, certain relatives, places we had lived, most of the past, politics, foreign affairs – or without wading into the oceans of forgetfulness and obliviousness that had built up around things she once cared about and I still did – books, films, the news. But if I told her what I was cooking for friends over the weekend, we would fall into a safe place together, one where past, present and future were full of afternoons in the kitchen with the radio on and with chocolate-smeared mixing bowls in the sink, desserts cooling in the refrigerator, sauces simmering on the stove, a slowly crisping, caramelizing roast in the oven and the house full of mingling, delicious smells.

It was the lovely afternoon of 4 May 2005. The pink bunched flowers of the horse chestnut tree outside her window in Swiss Cottage swayed gently in a spring breeze. She had not cooked for a long time, having moved from a studio flat where she would at best fry some bacon, to a locked mental ward in an industrial corner of north-west London, and then to this charming, sunlit room on the top floor of an old people's home called Rathmore House, where she was a teenager compared to the dying bodies who sat immobile in the hallway. She was closer in age to some of the staff than to the other residents, and she didn't socialize with the bent-over old ladies who stared into their ever-dimming memories. Unlike them, she would walk along the street to the local shops and cafés, sitting with a cup of coffee and making friends with the local misfits who also spent their days over coffee. She kept to her room when in the home. She read the occasional novel, watched television and waited for phone calls and visits from my sister and me.

She hated the food there, that was the only thing, and loved to be taken out. A few days earlier, on a walk to the shops of nearby Primrose Hill with my sister, she had bought me a present. It was a zester, and she handed it to me now without wrapping paper or reason. She knew I would like it. I had another zester already, but immediately I liked this one more. It had a solid ball of steel for a handle. She had bought an identical one for my sister.

She stood up from her armchair and we kissed and I hugged her, smiling. It was an unplanned visit, an hour snatched because I happened to be at home in London rather than in a war zone and I was passing by. It had been an hour without my getting irritated, one in which I asked for and received rare

2

maternal advice about things I have already forgotten because it was the unwonted feeling of being looked after by my mother that mattered. The zester, bought by chance in a shop on the same street as the flat where a young Elizabeth David, my mother's cooking guru, first began to cook for herself, was in my hand as I hugged her.

I put it into my pocket and left.

She died two days later, in the morning, in that room. She fell forward on to the floor in front of her armchair, her heart stopping without warning.

2

By the time I was eighteen years old, I wanted my mother, who had brought me into the world and deluged me with love, to die. And I said so, out loud.

I stood in the kitchen of my aunt's apartment in Newport, Rhode Island, where I was staying for the summer, saving my tips and pay cheques from the job I had in a restaurant clearing tables so that I could spend the autumn and winter travelling around the United States on Greyhound buses. It was the summer of 1988. My aunt Jennifer was two years older than my mother. They were the oldest of four siblings and had been extremely close when they were children.

My aunt emigrated from Scotland to the United States, to Boston, the year John Kennedy was assassinated. I had just finished secondary school in Scotland, and when I joined my aunt in this fresh, exciting country, I found in her something that I had not known for years. She was like my mother in so many ways – her voice, her eyes, her sporadic disdain for decorum. When she had met me off the bus in Providence on my first day in the States, she had parked illegally, and when we rushed back to her car she began an argument with the meek-looking uniformed attendant who must have been earning just over the minimum wage in his middle years and whom my lovely aunt loudly called 'a Nazi'. My mother would have done that. But they were different in other ways. Unlike my mother, Jennifer did actually come to pick me up from the bus station; she would do my laundry, watch films with me, make me coffee, share my jokes, treat me to dinner out. She did not argue with me. I could talk with her without constantly censoring myself. When my cousin Christian pierced my ear with a needle and thread and a block of ice, my aunt handed me a brandy from her freezer.

And now, in the afternoon before my evening shift at the wharf-side restaurant in Newport where I worked, as illegal as my Salvadoran buddies, we were talking about my mother.

'I don't think I've ever told anyone this,' I said, 'but I think she'd be better off dead.'

'So do I,' she said.

There was a moment of quiet.

'Matthew,' she said, reaching for the freezer, 'would you like a brandy?'

'I think she'd be happier dead,' I said, taking the glass. 'She's never going to get better. She just suffers. Her life is worthless.'

And it was unspoken, but understood, that it would be easier and better for me, and for everyone else in the family.

I had had, in many ways, an idyllic childhood. But that seemed many years ago now, and I felt that on many levels it had been a lie, or a promise of a future that was then snatched from me for ever. Throughout my teenage years I had increasingly come to feel that my parents had set me up for a fall. My first ten years had been good to live but were now unbearable to remember. I had begun to close the valve on that particular stream of memories.

'You shouldn't feel guilty for feeling that, you know,' Jennifer said.

'I don't,' I said. And, in my blind teenage rage, I really didn't.

My mother did not die then. But many years later she said to me: 'I'm ready to die now, Matty. I've been married, I've had my children. I'm ready to die.'

She was not depressed when she said this. She wasn't drunk or ranting. We were having a cup of tea in her small basement studio flat in Kilburn, in north-west London, a five-minute amble from my sister's place, the last place she would live without full-time carers on hand. She repeated it to me at other times, in moments of calm and relative serenity. My sister told me she had heard the same. 'I've read enough books,' she said. 'I've planted enough flowers and cooked enough meals. I'm not interested in that stuff any more.'

By then I no longer considered her life worthless, but I respected her readiness to die. She had reached an end, I supposed. So it was fine with me.

And then she died on a Friday morning, while I was having breakfast alone in a café, reading the newspaper. I walked home and my sister called, her voice afraid and small. 'Mum's dead,' she said. And after I called my father, who had not spoken with my mother for many years, and her siblings, and a funeral director I plucked from the Yellow Pages, and the coroner's office to ask where my mother actually was – an ambulance and police officers had come to the home to take her away – and when her body would be available for collection by the funeral director, I sat at the table in my flat and my body began to shake.

It was absolutely not fine for my mother to be dead. The feeling began at the base of my torso, to the rear, and moved up like nausea through my chest. When it hit my head, it distorted my face and contracted my throat into wails and squeezed my eyes. And it stayed there for about two hours, the waves of its storm growing taller each time, so that I had to drink glasses of water to compensate for the stuff pouring out of my eyes and nose. It left me exhausted and staring at nothing, until I began to feel I was recovering, and then it came back up from the base of my spine, again and again and again. For days. For weeks. For months.

3

In the first days after my mother's death, before her funeral, much of my brain seemed to close down, my thoughts reduced to two simple sentences, which repeated themselves over and over.

'Where are you? Please come back.'

I ran through the parks of north-west London, through the long grass of May, and one morning, midway through a lap of nearby Queen's Park, I found myself repeating a third sentence, an unexpected mantra of panic, speaking it aloud through my tears as I ran. 'Dad, please don't die.'

The last defence I had left in the world. I needed someone, after all, to look after me. It was inconceivable, unimaginable that I could be left to fend for myself. I was surprised at my terror. I had been self-sufficient, in a relatively intense way, for many years. And I had been in some alarming places and situations. But I had never been so afraid as now.

I ran back home and stood in my living room, sweating in my T-shirt and shorts, trying to keep my voice under control, dialling my father's number.

'Hi, Matt,' he said, his voice at its gentlest. 'How are you doing?'

'Dad,' I said, 'I don't want you to die.'

I was thirty-five years old and I felt like a very small boy. My mother had not looked after me, had not protected me, for about a quarter of a century. And yet I knew with a terrifying certainty that half of the protective field that some part of me relied on instinctively to keep me safe and to make sense of the world had been wiped out for ever.

At the age of seven I had sat with her on a rock overlooking the sea near our house on the west coast of Scotland. The grey waves heaved in from the Atlantic, whitening on the barnacle-studded shelf of rock along the coast, an outcrop that would rip apart any boat that came close to it, any sailor who fell in. The place still scares me, the hidden depths of kelp and power churning unseen beneath the rock shelf. I leaned against the green canvas coat my mother wore.

'What would you do if I fell in?' I asked.

'I'd go in after you,' she said, without hesitating.

'But you'd die,' I said, not entirely believing her because it simply didn't make sense. 'You would drown too.'

'Maybe. But I'd still go in after you.' She squeezed me in her arms. I stared at the waves for a little longer and then held open her hands, comparing their size to mine, liking the grit under her fingernails and the chafing and cuts and toughness she picked up when we were in Ardnamurchan for several weeks.

'I wouldn't go in after you,' I said, looking back at the impossible walls of water whose spray reached our Wellington boots.

That woman had been long gone. By the time my mother died, she had not been in a position to jump in after me for many years. But her love was just as furious and unremitting. Without it, it seemed, I was useless. The initial burst of phone calls I made after hearing about my mother's death was followed by paralysis. My sister had to call the lawyer and the priest. She had to design and print the order of service for the funeral and choose the hymns. She had to get a removal firm to take away my mother's possessions from the home and put them in storage somewhere. She had to return calls to the coroner, who was making sure our mother hadn't been murdered in her old people's home; indeed, she had died only of a heart attack, my sister reported. My sister had to fetch some clothes

– a denim dress – for my mother to wear in her coffin. My sister was dynamic; I was stuck. I couldn't call people back. I couldn't write thank-you notes when letters of condolence arrived. I couldn't look after my girlfriend, who was in hospital recovering from an operation when my mother died. I could go to the pub and embarrass myself in public with my tears. I could choose a song for the end of the funeral. I could write a eulogy. That was about it.

'It's like walking along the road and someone walking up to you and punching you in the face, really hard, for no reason,' I told friends who had not had a parent die. 'I'm telling you, I just want you to know, when it happens it'll take you by surprise. It will totally shock you.' They nodded but I knew they had no idea of what lay ahead, for the death of a parent is an event for which there is no preparation. You can't lose your mother or father twice.

But the punch analogy was slightly off. It was more like a scene from a Robin Hood film. You're trotting along through the forest on your horse when a swinging sack of wheat sweeps silently through the trees and broadsides you. And then you are utterly winded, motionless, undefended, staring at the insects and the pine cones on the forest floor. All the life and breath gone from you.

On the Saturday morning after my mother died, I went with my sister to the funeral director's in Notting Hill. The man, John, was kind in a studied fashion: like his colleague on the phone the night before, he referred to my mother, a woman he had never met, as 'Mum'. As in: 'We'll get Mum from the coroner on Monday.' And: 'What sort of coffin would you like for Mum?' And: 'Did Mum want to be buried or cremated?'

As we walked home, my sister and I passed the stalls selling falafel and chorizo on Golborne Road and we came to one of the eclectic antique shops there. I went in and saw a huge stuffed wildebeest head mounted on the wall.

'How much is the wildebeest?' I asked the man in the shop.

The stuffed wildebeest bust was enormous. It would protrude far into any room I was likely to live in as if craning over a stable door. I could already see it in place in my flat.

'Six hundred pounds.'

I turned to my sister. 'I lost my mother; I'm going to get a consolation wildebeest.'

'Why don't you give that a bit more thought,' she said, and steered me out of the shop.

4

The coroner released my mother's body to the funeral director. The paramedics had taken her from her room to the coroner. People I had never met were passing my mother around from fridge to fridge, from trolley to trolley. I felt like taking her home and laying her out on my dining table, for an old-fashioned peasant wake. She would still be in my possession. I could invite everyone round and serve them glasses of undiluted whisky. But it doesn't work that way. You have to go to what is, essentially, a shop to see your dead. So on the evening before the funeral, my sister, my girlfriend – back home from hospital – and I sat for a few moments in the wood-panelled anteroom of the funeral home I had randomly chosen, on Ladbroke Grove, waiting to see my mother's body. I thought: 'She must have had her chest sliced open and poked around in by the coroner. She must have the most enormous slice down her torso, all sewn up in perhaps not the most cosmetically careful way.'

'Have you ever seen a dead body before?' I asked my sister and girlfriend, while John made sure that 'Mum' was ready for us.

'No,' they said.

I thought of saying something comforting. I had some experience of death and dead bodies. I thought of my first encounter with violent death. I was standing on a subway station platform in Boston, on the Red Line, in late 1993 as I made my way to teach an introductory writing course to undergraduates at the college I was attending as a graduate

11

student in Worcester, Massachusetts. It was very early in the morning. The train came into the station. The unshaven man ten feet to my left stumbled towards the edge of the platform. Just before the train got to him, he fell in front of it and disappeared from sight. The train cut him in half, I learned later.

That was just chance; then the observation of dead bodies became part of my job. My first actual view of a dead body was the following year, 1994. I was doing work experience as a reporter at *Newsday*, the Long Island newspaper. The news editor sent me to a road called Sunrise Highway. A motorcyclist had been showing off to his friends on the dual carriageway. He was balancing his helmet on his forehead, the police explained to me; it slipped on to his nose and, suddenly blinded, he rode into the back of a parked truck. 'That's what we call a cleansing-the-gene-pool story, Matty,' said Lucinda, a reporter who covered the police, when I came back to the office after staring transfixed at the man's brains drooping on to the road.

From early 1999 onward, I saw a lot of dead people in war zones. Some of them, in Kosovo and Iraq, had been dug up from mass graves and were in various states of decomposition. Others were the brand-new dead, their bullet holes fresh on their sallow skin. I particularly remembered a Palestinian boy in a morgue in Nablus, in the West Bank; some of his bones poked out from his skin, white and obscene. He was about ten and had been playing outside the local Hamas political offices when a couple of Israeli rockets turned up to decapitate the Hamas leaders – whom I knew – inside the building. He wore white underpants and nothing else. Then there were the ambulances and morgues of Baghdad, full up with what remained of the latest group of civilians who had been hit by a suicide bomb.

But none of the dead I had seen had been my mother. They did not help me nor did they qualify me to be reassuring to anyone else. I said nothing.

John appeared from the viewing room in the back.

'Would Mum have been wearing lipstick?' he asked.

'Er, no,' my sister, Jane, said.

'I didn't think so,' John said. 'I don't know how it got there. I'll just remove it.'

Sometime between my mother's keeling over dead, being cut up on the coroner's slab and being dressed up in the funeral home, someone had decided she needed a makeover.

John disappeared and, after a few moments, came back.

'OK,' he said.

Despite John's best efforts with a Kleenex or baby wipe, I could still detect traces of a vibrant red on my mother's lips, which were stretched wide across her cheeks as if she had a very big mouth. The lips were not grimacing or smiling, just stretched; I had not seen that expression on my mother's face before.

'She's so small,' I said. She lay in her coffin – not a fancy one – and wore her denim dress.

When I was a boy I would put empty potato crisp packets in my mother's oven for a few seconds until they had shrunk to minute versions of themselves. My mother looked like that: oven-shrunk.

'Beautiful Mummy,' Jane said, and we both cried. Jane gently stroked my mother's greying hair, which lay flat on her forehead.

'Beautiful Mummy.'

It scared me to touch her. I had seen all those dead people, but I realized I had never touched any of them.

We stayed for some time and I didn't want to leave her. I wanted to sit down and lean against the wall and fall asleep for the night. Because to me, this was my mother. It was not just my mother's body. I had no God, no religion, no sense of life after death. I sensed no spirit, no soul; no smiling, released, protective, newly omnipotent mother looking down on us. All I had was this lifeless body we were getting ready to burn. I had only a few hours left to spend with her.

13

But we left.

I sat next to my father at the funeral, the hymns leaving me cold, the liturgy passing me by unnoticed, the wooden box parked in the aisle to my left the only thing I cared about. I touched it with my left hand as I passed it by on my way to give the eulogy. I stood at the lectern, gazing out at the immigrant African and elderly Irish Catholics who, besides those who had come to mourn for my mother, seemed to make up the bulk of the regular congregation.

Until she died, I had not known that this church, the Sacred Heart Church on Quex Road in Kilburn, a ten-minute walk from my flat, was where my mother had been christened during the Second World War. I had not known, in fact, that she was born in London. I had, over the years, become almost allergic to her past. I did not want to hear stories of the past, because for me they were all stories of pain and loss.

Sixty-two years earlier my mother had been held in her own mother's arms on this spot, her forehead dampened with holy water.

I stood at the lectern and read my way, with some effort, through this:

I've been trying to fill up the hours since Mum died, and so one day last week I found a site on the Internet that was all about babies' names and I stuck the name Ann into the site's search engine. I wanted to know what Ann meant. Hebrew for gracious, came the answer. So then I thought a bit about what gracious really means and I realized that I wasn't sure, so the dictionary gave me several definitions; one of them was this: characterized by tact and propriety. If the name Ann, I thought, implies being characterized by tact, then I think Granny and Grandpa seriously misnamed my mother. My mum was perhaps the least tactful person I've ever known. Even when she was a young woman, before she fell ill, I'm told that she had quite a capacity to embarrass and offend.

14

And yet my dad fell in love with her, her siblings adored her and she had an army of wonderful friends. And no matter what she did to embarrass or irritate Jane and me, we loved her.

You see, that tactlessness was actually a good thing – it was a brilliant, attractive lack of inhibition that enabled her to cut through the nonsense and get to the point. My friend Rich told me last week that he used to come round to my house when we were difficult teenagers and my mum, unlike any other parent, would treat him like an adult, talking to him without condescension.

It was that almost total lack of inhibition that enabled her to radiate love in that extraordinarily passionate and penetrating, very public way of hers. It meant that I grew up in a home where we said 'I love you' to each other all the time; where I used to kiss my dad on his cheeks, nose, forehead, chin and lips every night before I went to bed; where I wanted to marry my sister because I loved her so much. And I think we three all learned that from my mum. I certainly did, and even though she's gone now, I'll always try to keep her particular sort of passionate and uninhibited love in my life.

A bit later in her life, things got in the way of my mum loving those around her quite as well as she had done before. As a secret Jewish envoy to Ireland, she had to bring an end to the conflict there. As the heiress to both the Romanov and Hapsburg empires, she had a lot of letters to write. My mum had a lot on her plate.

Sadly, in the course of her missions and her drinking and madness, she pushed away many of friends and family members.

But it was her illness that made her angry and hurtful; it was not her. A huge malfunction took hold of her brain and became as much of a burden to her as anything to anyone I have ever seen. And this is what actually makes me so admire her, makes me so miss her, makes me love her so much even now – because, apart from one attempt at suicide, for which I am sure she was long ago forgiven, she never gave up. She had so little to live for for so long and she kept fighting, and she must have known something that I didn't, because, at various points, I thought she'd be better off dead. I was wrong. A sort of miracle happened. With the help of her treasured, limitlessly giving daughter, Jane, and her own sheer determination, Mum found happiness and love and a sort of sanity again. I've never managed to show such strength, such courage, such resilience, such hope, such a refusal to take the easy option. I've never fought against such odds. But my little, damaged mother fought and she won. In that sense, it wasn't a miracle at all. It was not something that happened to her. She made it happen. It was a choice, a very difficult one – and all I can say is that I hope to be able to remember her hard choice for the rest of my life and to remind myself of it when faced with difficult decisions and challenges.

Mum's choice was this: to get better, and to keep loving. In the past few years, she lived up to her name again. She was gracious. Other definitions offered by the dictionary: characterized by charm or beauty, by elegance and good taste, by kindness and warm courtesy; of a merciful or compassionate nature.

She told Jane and me that she was ready to die. Well, we were absolutely not ready to lose her. We had our charming, beautiful, elegant, tasteful, kind, warm and compassionate mum back. But now she's gone and so all I can do is to feel her with me somehow, in some way, and to look at a final, archaic definition of gracious: enjoying favour or grace; acceptable or pleasing.

I hope she is enjoying favour with her God, that she is as acceptable and pleasing as she is no doubt tactless, wandering around heaven, loudly making friends with whomever she comes across, loving her children and all of you from afar with the same passion she loved us with while she was here.

My eulogy, I should say, contained three inaccuracies. First, her recovery was not quite as complete as I suggested in the church. Second, I didn't buy any of the heaven stuff – but this was her funeral, not mine, and she believed in a heaven that we all go to. Third, I didn't feel her with me in the slightest. She was very much not with me, not then and, I was sure, not ever again.

We drove to the crematorium in a fleet of minicabs. I almost lost my temper with our driver, and when we reached the crematorium there was no one to direct us to the correct chapel. Finally we found it and filed in. The coffin had preceded us and was sitting in front of a red curtain. The priest, a kind, soft-voiced Indian from Kerala named Father Benny, said the final words:

'Take something of Ann with you in your hearts when you go.'

Perhaps it was a standard funeral line. But it felt to me as though Father Benny, soon to return to his native India, had understood that my mother had been complicated but good, that there was a lot of my mother you would not want to take away with you in your heart but a lot that you would. The coffin rolled through the curtains.

The tapas at the pub dining room where we held the wake were delicious. I had been able to help with that part of the arrangement.

Sack races in the garden at Ashworth Road in London

5

On a quiet morning, I stood on a bridge over the canal in Little Venice with an umbrella keeping me dry. The late spring rain pattered on the surface of this waterway that bends its way from west to east London, hidden for much of the way by homes and warehouses and tunnels. I was early for my appointment with the therapist whose office was in the tall, white-painted Georgian house overlooking the canal. I had stood here before, over thirty years ago, holding my mother's hand as I looked down through the metal railings at one of the broad, low boats that take tourists through the city. I must have been two or three years old. It is the first thing I remember.

But I had few other recollections of London, purely because I was too young to remember much. We left when I was three, for Edinburgh, where I grew up. My memories of Edinburgh also featured black holes, but these were, I suspect, more a result of unconscious self-preservation. For instance, Jane once told me about how our mother, babbling incoherently, had shown up at our schools in the middle of the day, when I was about ten, and had tried to drive us away 'to somewhere lovely and safe where you'll be happy' without telling our father. The car had been packed rather haphazardly, with things like our teddy bears clearly visible. Jane had grown quickly suspicious and while our mother was getting my teacher to take me out of class she had made a run for it, to a nearby phone box, and had hidden there until Dad had arrived. To my surprise, I had only the barest flicker of memory when Jane told me this even though she said 'we were both pretty shaken by the whole thing'.

After Edinburgh and university I moved to the United States and soon after became a newspaper reporter. My newspaper sent me to the Middle East, Northern Ireland, the Balkans, and I went gladly; went just about anywhere there was a conflict, anywhere I could dive into the pain of others and feel alive and invigorated by the most extreme experiences human beings go through.

After the invasion of Iraq and the increasingly bloody summer of 2003, however, an unstoppable impulse returned me to London, a city that I barely knew but that now seemed like the only place in the world I could live. My mother, my sister, my closest friends all lived in London. This was where my family, many years before, had been whole and happy. But though I had now lived there for over a year, it was still a city I barely knew, because for much of that time I had been in Iraq or another country. I still needed the A–Z to find my way around, to find the neighbourhood where I'd spent my first three years. I knew Jerusalem and Baghdad much better than I knew London.

I turned my eyes from the water and moved towards the large white house. The trees along the canal were the yellow-green of high spring, and I had an urge to touch them and be surrounded by greenery. I had been running a lot in recent days, searching out the lushest, most life-filled parks I could find. I wanted to roll in deep grass. I wanted to lie down sideways at the top of a grassy slope and roll down, over and over, until I'd reach the bottom all dizzy and be steadied by my mother, who would be waiting there.

I had not met the therapist before, but I knew he was a former foreign correspondent, which meant that there would be so much less to explain. He had helped other war-buffeted correspondents, their numbers growing quickly in the years of unending conflict since the attacks of 11 September 2001, and

I was hoping he could help me. I had an important assignment for my newspaper coming up, and I needed to be a bit more functional than I was.

We sat down in his office and he asked how he could help me. He was immediately likeable.

'I'm supposed to go on a trip to Nepal, to track down the Maoists, and I don't know if I really feel up to it,' I said. I had not made a single phone call. I had not set up a single interview. I was leaving very soon. 'It's not as though it's dangerous there, but I don't really want to go.'

'How long's the trip?'

'A month or so. I'm kind of exhausted. I mean, loads of us are in this situation, the post-9/11 endless-war thing. Afghanistan, Iraq, you know. Perhaps I have post-traumatic stress disorder.'

'Are you having flashbacks or nightmares?'

'Not really.'

'Do you get irrationally angry?'

'Sometimes.'

He didn't look too worried about me. Perhaps his being a former correspondent made him wise to the whining of someone who had chosen, entirely of his own accord, to do what was essentially a very stupid job.

To me, my gloom seemed to have this screamingly obvious source: cumulative war, perhaps accented by my mother's death.

The battle of Fallujah, in which I had been embedded with American troops, had taken place only seven months beforehand, in November 2004. It had been the most intense combat the US military had engaged in since the Vietnam War. It had been particularly terrifying.

'Also,' I said, 'my mother died three weeks ago.'

'Oh,' said the therapist, his face shifting with sudden interest. 'No wonder you feel terrible. I'm so sorry.'

I told him about wanting to be surrounded by greenery. He said that was common. I didn't tell him about the wildebeest.

I filled out a questionnaire designed to test whether I had the symptoms of post-traumatic stress disorder, and the results showed that I was perfectly OK. The source of my virtual paralysis had nothing to do with war, he said. The problem was a bit less glamorous and quite ordinary, really: my mum was dead.

I was surprised by his conclusion. All mothers die sooner or later, don't they?

'There's some research that's shown that mothers and sons have particularly close bonds,' the therapist told me. 'This is going to be very difficult.'

I appreciated his sympathy and his insistence that my sadness was to be expected, but I still felt that my recent howling, animalistic fits of grief were disproportionate, that they somehow didn't match up to what had just happened. I had lost my mother – an extremely common event that conformed to the natural sequence of life and death. Billions of mothers had died. Millions, I supposed, died every year. Even if sons and mothers are particularly close – and I suspect fathers and daughters and mothers and daughters might contest that – a son's losing his mother was one of the world's great unoriginal misfortunes. Besides, parents are meant to go before their children. And at sixty-two, my mother, who had lived an unhealthy life for decades, was not exceptionally young to die. Off and on, I had been expecting her death for more than half of my own life. Once, in 1994, I grieved for her even though she was still alive.

One of her letters had arrived in the ground-floor letterbox of the small flat I shared on the fourth floor of an East Village tenement building. When these letters came, sometimes several in one day, I would feel a heaviness come over me, and a noticeable dialling down of energy – even if I didn't open them, which I often didn't. When I did, I would erect a kind of emotional forcefield around myself as my fingers peeled open the envelope. I needed to be able to read them without feeling too much. One from that time begins: 'Matty darling – I'm trying to propagate my new <u>Society for the Improvement of the Universe</u>. I want Jen to do it – could you give her a prod – she's lazy. If she won't do it – wld C or S [my cousins Christian and Sarah, who also live in Newport] – it would be good if the young do it. All you need is a group of brainy *imaginative* – that's essential – people – different races – religions – political ideas etc. – to meet to discuss ideas & how to implement them.' The letter ends: 'Think about Liberation Theology & the Parable of the Talents. KISSES Mummy.' In other letters she refers to this 'Society' as her 'international think-tank'.

For some years she had pronounced at various times that I was the hidden king of the Austro-Hungarian Empire, that she was the Tsarina, that we were Jewish, that I would inevitably be prime minister, that she was advising various governments on how to resolve the great challenges of the era and warning them of fascist or nationalist threats. She did, in fact, make contact with those at the highest level of government.

'The Prime Minister has asked me to thank you for your recent letter,' John Major's correspondence secretary wrote to my mother in March 1996, politely fobbing off whatever nutty enquiry she had made.

'I have read your points with interest and certainly share your views on the importance of the family,' writes Michael Ancram, a Scottish Conservative MP, to my mother in December 1995.

'Your letter of 6 March addressed to Mrs Blair has been passed to me,' Alistair Darling, who was later to become Chancellor of the Exchequer, dictates to his secretary on 18 March 1996. 'Mrs Blair is a private individual and does not become involved in matters which are more properly the province of politics.'

I don't recall what the particular letter that I received on this day in 1994 said – my memory seems to have closed that off for ever – but it felled me. I sat on a fold-up chair in my small bedroom and sobbed, occasionally stuffing my face into my pillow to prevent any neighbours hearing. My two flat-mates were out, fortunately. Eventually I called my sister, in London.

'I just feel that Mum is basically dead,' I said, 'and even though I've told myself for ages that that's just the way things are I'm having these waves of grief. I had this amazing mum and I miss her.'

'Oh Matt,' my sister said, 'I know.'

'Other people grow up with mums but I've had that stolen from me. Other people can call their mums for a chat or for advice. We'll never get her back, you know. It keeps hitting me, this sudden grief.'

The grief passed but it struck me now, more than ten years later, that that day in New York had given me a glimpse of what I might one day be faced with should my mother ever actually die. No wonder I had closed down so many memories and thoughts of her, to the point where sometimes she barely existed to me. Now she really was dead. And it flummoxed me.

The therapist suggested two ways I might help myself. I should read some books on grieving, and I should know, impossible as it might now seem to me, that time tempers grief. The first anniversary would likely be punishing; the second surprisingly less so. I thanked him and walked along the canal in the rain to buy dinner in the shops on Clifton Road where my mother used to shop when I was a baby.

6

A week later I was in the skies above the Kathmandu Valley, the plane swooping down through the clouds to a city that seemed calm but was teetering on the verge of catastrophe. Nepal was a country of one anachronism piled on top of another, where an autocratic king was considered by his more religious and loyal subjects to be a reincarnation of the Hindu god Vishnu and where some of the country's dispossessed had taken to the hills in a Maoist insurgency.

It took three and a half days of hiking through the hills, treading through paddy fields and alongside rivers, to reach the Maoist capital of Thabang, which was really just a slightly larger village than most others in the region.

In the evening, I asked the most senior Maoist leader in the town about his plans for the new society that he and his comrades would create once the revolution was victorious. We sat in a dark room and he promised me they would be merciful when they took Kathmandu.

And then it was three and a half days back along the same path, single-file hiking for hour after hour. When it rained we sheltered under rocks. When we reached the end of each morning, we found a guest house where we slept for an hour and ate rice and dhal off metal plates. In one place, close by a river, we ate finger-sized fish, and the rice was flavoured with hot lemon pickle.

We took our boots and trousers off and waded into the strong river, rubbing three days of sweat from our bodies as the sun baked our faces.

In the rhythm and the repetition of those days of walking and refuelling on rice, my messy grief sorted itself out so that all that was left was the same question and plea that had first appeared in my mind in the confusion of immediate grief. There was a clarity to it now. I wanted to know where my mother was, and I wanted her to come back.

I was surprised by the persistence of these two thoughts. I knew she was gone for ever and I knew she wasn't coming back. But that seemed unbearable. I had to do something to find out where she was and to bring her back to me. I needed to work to find a solution. We hiked back to where the road began and made our way back to Kathmandu.

My sister is not a religious person, but right from the start she felt our mother with her, watching over her. When I returned to London I told her that I had no way of feeling the same.

'Sometimes I just slip into this little church on Farm Street in Mayfair,' she said. My sister worked in an art gallery in central London, and the church was a short walk from the gallery. 'It's a Catholic church and it's really pretty, really small. There's a little chapel there – to Our Lady of Lourdes – and for some reason I'm just drawn to it. I know Mum went to the church sometimes, but I don't know if she went to that chapel. I light candles for her. I feel very close to her there. You could try going there. Besides, it's round the corner from the best butcher in London.'

'OK,' I said, and forgot about it.

I called my aunt Kata, my mother's younger sister. Kata was the person my mother talked to most, other than Jane and me.

'I miss Mum,' I said, crinkling into silent tears as soon as I had said it.

'I miss your mother terribly,' she said. 'But I talk to her every day. I talk to them all, to her and Mummy and Daddy. She sits on the sofa. She's very bossy. She can be quite cruel sometimes.'

'You mean you actually talk to her and see her?' I asked.

'Yes,' she said. 'I know it sounds crazy, but it's true.'

My sofa remained unvisited. My sister reminded me a couple of times about the Farm Street church, but it had no draw for me.

Was this what happened to the Godless when faced with grief? Sudden, irreversible motherlessness until you die. Atheism's toll. The shocking lack of consolation only made me hunger further for a way back to her.

After my visit to the therapist, I had gone to a bookshop and found an entire section devoted to grief and mourning. I bought three books, and when I got home I looked briefly at two of them.

I'd known about Elisabeth Kübler-Ross's groundbreaking work and her description of the five stages that follow death: denial and isolation; anger; bargaining; depression; acceptance. Now, even glancing at this carefully mapped-out route to feeling better and accepting the unacceptable made me close the book in irritation.

The second book focused on the death of parents. It was full of real-life anecdotes about dead mothers and fathers. But there was, of course, nothing in there about my own dead mother; I found myself entirely uninterested in anyone else's. I didn't want to read about 'coping' and 'reassessing' a dead parent and 'how you may feel'. I did not want to cope or come to terms with my mother's death.

The book discussed the two-year anniversary. The idea of my mother's death reaching me like a ripple from a distant storm, easy and fading after two years, was not appealing. It's not that I was enjoying the pain, but I didn't want it to fade. The pain was a link to my mother. It was the pain that was driving me to find a concrete way to be with my mother again.

Only one line I came across in my reading seemed addressed to me. The author had borrowed it from J. William Worden, an influential grief therapist: 'For many, two years is not too long.'

When I thought of my mother in those moments of wishing her back, I did not often picture the greying, false-teeth-wearing, puffy-faced woman of sixty-two who had recently died. I longed for a woman who had not really existed for twenty-five years. I mourned for a young, beautiful, happy woman I could remember only in fragments. That just made my yearning all the more absurd, but it was nonetheless insistent. How to get back a woman who had not breathed for a quarter of a century?

7

My mother holds a pin in her right hand. Her eyes are closed.
She is standing in front of a map of the west coast of Scotland
spread out on a table. She and my father, having left their
home in London for a short holiday, are in the basement of
her parents' house in Edinburgh. Her hand moves through the
air, and the pin pierces the paper of the map. My parents bend
down to look where it has landed. The pin is in the sea near a
village called Kilchoan on a peninsula called Ardnamurchan.
The land mass sticks out from the ragged coastline, pointing
directly to the west. Its tip is the westernmost point of main-
land Britain.

It is the summer of 1969 and I am a few months away from
being born. I'm a bulge in my mother's belly. My grandmother
has agreed to look after my sister, Jane, who is not quite two
years old, for a week while my parents visit friends on the west
coast.

Before they go to visit their friends, they want a little time
on their own, and the pin-in-the-map game is their way of
choosing where to go. They pack up their car and head
north, past the ancient castle on the hill at Stirling, across
the water-soaked plateau of Rannoch Moor and through
the glacier-scooped valley of Glencoe, until they are driving
along a single-lane road hugging the shore of the fjord that
is Loch Sunart. They're proceeding towards the point where
the pin landed, towards the tiny Kilchoan Hotel. Along the
way they meet cars head-on and are forced to reverse into

the intermittent bulges in the narrow road that have been designed to allow cars to pass each other. My father quickly learns the local ways, raising a hand or a finger or nodding his head or smiling in thanks when other cars reverse for him. For one stretch, the road passes through a mass of rhododendron bushes, purpling the dark, dense green of the trees on the southern coast of this peninsula. And then up through one final shady glade and suddenly they're driving in a landscape almost completely without trees, as the road veers north across the land, through the peat and the heather and the volcanic rocks warming in the sunshine. Below them in a bay named Camas nan Geall is a sandy beach and fields that are home to a Bronze Age burial chamber and a standing stone engraved with a cross; it is said the early Christian missionaries St Columba and St Ciaran came to the bay as they spread Christianity to this part of Scotland. The burial chamber is where St Ciaran is believed to be buried. Above my mother and father as they drive around the rim of the bay are the dark-green slopes of a peak that falls away into the sea. They pass a loch on their right, and at the same time the view opens up ahead of them and there is the northern side of the peninsula and the blue-grey Atlantic and the overlapping islands of Eigg, Muck, Rum, Canna, Skye. Canna is so flat that it appears as a shelf just above the horizon. Skye's high mountains form a crocodile's spine in the clouds.

My parents have come from their home in London for a few days of this empty, beautiful place. At the Kilchoan Hotel, the landlord cares about food and wine, and my parents are surprised to eat so well.

When they go out to explore the countryside around them, they drive along the roads of the peninsula, pulling their car over whenever something catches their eye. Leaving the car behind, they walk into the hills or they meander along the sands at Sanna, where the waves come straight in from the Atlantic and crash on to the beach in white spray, catching the sun.

31

Even in midsummer, the whole peninsula of Ardnamurchan is almost deserted.

One day they are on the road to a place signposted Fascadale, its name a poem in itself, and they pull on to a patch of grass alongside the road. There is a rising hill behind them, covered in heather and bracken and spindly oak trees that can never become fully grown because of the north wind and the salt it carries with it. The sea stretches in front of them, blue and grey, cresting with white. The air is not just clean and fresh but it seems to open up parts of them that the city has kept closed. They lie down on a patch of grass and stare at the blue sky, and my father thinks that this is the most magical place he has ever been to. It is not an easy place, not lush, not sun-smoothed. The coastline squares up, ragged and dark, to confront the furious Atlantic. My mother's belly forms a hillock on my father's horizon. They return to the same spot the next day and lie down again and look at the sky again and the feeling is the same. Perhaps, they say to each other, we should move here.

The sixties are almost over by the summer of their first visit to Ardnamurchan. My parents had watched the decade rather than participated in it. They are a bit scared of drugs. They own one Beatles LP, one Joplin record and nothing by Hendrix, the Who, the Rolling Stones, the Doors, or Cream. They see films and plays but not rock concerts. My mother does like the clothes of the era, shopping at Mary Quant's first shop just south of Kensington High Street.

My father is an advertising photographer. He goes to a couple of scenester parties, one hosted by a well-known fashion photographer named Hans Feurer, with whom he shares an agent, but he feels out of place. He walks through Hyde Park on the day of the Rolling Stones concert, 5 July 1969, stopping only to film some of the crowd and the rear of the stage with his cine camera. By coincidence, he is given a job in the summer of 1969, shortly before they go to Scotland, to photograph the cover of the new Rolling Stones record, *Let It Bleed*. His studio, usually his own domain, is taken over by the heroin-addicted designer Robert Brownjohn, best known for his title sequences for *Goldfinger* and *From Russia with Love*. Brownjohn, who will die a year later of a heart attack at the age of forty-four, bullies the cook my father has hired to bake the cake that will be featured on the cover. Her name is Delia Smith. Later she will become Britain's most successful TV chef, but on this day she is being ordered, unhappily, to produce ugly violet and green icing. There are a lot of people doing not very much in the studio other than getting in the way. For lunch, Brownjohn, Keith Richards, assorted hangers-on and my father head over to the fashionable Mario and Franco restaurant on Chancery Lane. The staff are highly suspicious of this gaggle until someone realizes that the man in the British Rail dining-car attendant's uniform is Keith Richards. The staff begin to fawn.

Over lunch my father persuades the excitable Brownjohn not to take a hammer to the cake when they get back to the studio but to allow him to mess it up a little more artfully for the back cover of the album. My father hates it all.

The only enjoyment he takes from that long day is when he and Richards realize they are both about to become fathers, Richards for the first time, my father for the second. My father finds Richards to be the only vaguely normal person at the table. It is the worst day of his working life thus far.

My parents go back to Ardnamurchan. After their initial visit in the summer of 1969, they spend months and then, on intermittent visits, years scouring the region for places to live, businesses to buy, routes out of urban living. Their friend Dominic is a partner in these escape plans. They consider buying the hotel where they first stayed. My mother would become a local teacher. They would harvest seaweed. They would buy a ruined crofting village, and my sister and I would grow up there amid the ghosts of the crofters pushed out during the Clearances. Dominic and my father would make a living from the sea – from a trawler, from lobster creels, from diving for scallops. One day, Dominic even persuades some local scallop divers to take him with them. When he reaches the floor of the sea loch and begins breathing ice-cold water into his lungs, he realizes that unless he kicks like hell he will die. Despite what he'd been told about the bends, he erupts like a submarine's missile from the surface of the sea loch. That is the end of that particular fantasy. Each plan blossoms over whisky and food and dies with time and testing.

So my parents scale back. They have already started looking for a piece of land on which to build a house where we can spend occasional long weekends and holidays. One day in late 1972, my father and Dominic, on one of the scouting missions that have taken them all over the west coast, are shown an isolated bay that is for sale by the local farmer. It is about four miles from where my parents first lay on their backs by the side of the road looking at the blue sky and wondering why they shouldn't live up there.

The farmer tells them the land is five acres and it is fine if my parents want to blast a half-mile-long track – it will take dynamite and some heavy machinery, he says – across his land to get down to the bay. There is no electricity, no telephone, and the only source of fresh water is a spring that sits downhill from the obvious spot to build a house. The bay is entirely sheltered by hills of heather, bracken, foxgloves and primroses and, closer to the sea, small cliffs and black rock, where sea pinks nestle in the furrows of the stone and flutter in the wind. It is a hidden place but broad and open and light. The land sweeps down to the sea.

The islands, eight miles away, fill the horizon.

My father and the farmer agree on a price immediately.

In 1973, my parents leave London for quieter, cheaper Edinburgh. In the land registry in Edinburgh, my mother finds out the bay's ancient Gaelic name: Port an Droighionn. It means port of the hawthorn or blackthorn. The only tree on the whole property is a stubborn, brave hawthorn that improbably stands on the edge of a small overhang in one of the most exposed corners of the bay. Perhaps it is a descendant of the old tree.

My father buys a used caravan and because the track hasn't yet been laid he has it dragged the half mile from the road across the peat bogs and the hills.

In these days before the track, everything has to be carried that half mile, including me. My father crouches down and leans forward, and I climb on to his back in my Wellington boots and pull myself on to his shoulders, using his forehead as leverage. I think it is funny to put my hands over his eyes and pull his sideburns as he lumbers through the peat bog and bracken, my own personal St Christopher.

My father buys a hand pump and some pipe and a large plastic water tank. He digs a hole next to the spring and sinks the tank into the earth. Then he lays a pipe that leads from the spot where the water bubbles out of the hill. The grey tank fills up with icy, clear, delicious water. With a lot of pulling and pushing of the pump's handle, the water creeps up the hill and into jerry cans.

We wash in the open air, naked as we are all day long whenever the sun shines.

On the two gas burners in the caravan, fuelled by a large orange Calor gas canister that sits outside, my mother fries slices of luncheon meat from the tin. She heats up tins of baked beans, tins of sweetcorn, tins of Fray Bentos steak pies, tins of tomato soup. Most things come from tins. After a day running around in the hills and the sea, it all tastes delicous. The milk is UHT or powdered, neither of which is even vaguely delicious.

We spend all our holiday time in Ardnamurchan, up to eight weeks at a stretch, the four of us (and sometimes our guests) living in that caravan. A man named Andrew blasts our track through the hills in May 1974, and in November of that year men come and build a Norwegian-designed log house. By the time we spend our first night in the house, in April 1975, Port an Droighionn has become more than home to us all.

Painting in the caravan at Port an Droighionn

8

The dark-green plastic urn full of my mother's ashes, a cheap-looking thing, sat in a back room in the funeral home for a few months until I took it to my flat in a cardboard box, which I stuffed into a yellow shopping bag from Selfridges. I stowed it next to my sofa, where it stayed until my sister and I could settle on a time to dispose of it properly, according to our mother's wishes.

It was about the weight of a couple of bricks.

On 24 September 2005 we took the train from London to Edinburgh. The urn went on the overhead baggage rack, on its side, and I hoped the lid was on firmly or my mother would start pouring out on to us and other passengers.

Some years earlier, my father had left Edinburgh for the countryside. But knowing that he would 'go nuts' in the isolation of Ardnamurchan, he moved to nearby Perthshire with his partner.

He had long since grown tired of being a photographer and was now a sculptor. Jane and I drove the forty-five minutes to their house, where we stayed the night. We kept the box in the boot of our car.

The next day we drove the five hours to Ardnamurchan, along the same road my parents had first taken in 1969.

My sister and I parked next to the house and I walked straight down to the shore, over the grass to the rocks and the sea filling the circular bay. The autumn afternoon breeze off the Atlantic had the last warmth of summer.

'Where are you?' I asked out loud. I wasn't expecting an apparition or a voice from the grave. I was hoping I might come up with an answer myself, in the way that a good idea or a clear memory sometimes arrived when I started writing, reading, focusing on a problem. None came. I picked up a large rock, lifted it over my head, and threw it down. Chips flew off it. I picked up the rock again and smashed it back on to the other rocks. It did not help. I felt silly.

My mother had not stayed a night in the house for more than two decades. In their divorce settlement, Port an Droighionn had gone to my father. She missed it terribly for the rest of her life. 'My beloved landscape,' she called it in a diary her psychiatric nurse asked her to write in 1991.

> The orchids, the lichen. The sea, the sky. The sunshine and the drizzle ... the midgety calm and the great gales. The figures that move through it, all beloved people, and the cows and the poor sheep, blamed for so much misery [during the Clearances]. I can't go there now, though I gave up my whole life for it ... Sad for the children, who must often be lonely and hungry there, and their mother isn't allowed to be there with them and for them, and to feed them. We built a house there, a pretty little wooden house ... How wonderful, how much-loved it was. I even cared for the lichen, the winkles. I used to pick the mussels off the shore and we used to eat them.

I put the box containing her ashes on the white Formica table in the kitchen where she had prepared a thousand meals.

My sister and I made dinner and invited Dominic. He had never lost his own love of the west coast and years earlier had built a log house about ten minutes' drive from ours. It was his full-time home. Like my father, he had not seen my mother, or talked with her, for many years. He had known her even before she met my father, when they were teenagers.

It was a simple meal, but one of the best quick recipes I

had come across: lamb mechoui, from the cooks at Moro, my favourite restaurant. I heated a griddle pan and made the mechoui salt, which is just some cumin seeds crushed in a mortar and pestle, some Maldon salt, some hot paprika and some sweet paprika. I melted some butter and coated the lamb chops we had brought with half of the spicy salt, then put them on the hot griddle pan.

As I cooked I noticed a small hole in one of the logs to the left of the cooker. In our early years up there, when we would spend the long summer holidays at Port an Droighionn, my father would buy two whole salamis from the Victor Hugo delicatessen in Edinburgh. One would be particularly large, with small fatty bits. The other was a little smaller and thinner, with glistening rounds of fat and peppercorns studding the meat. They would hang from the nail that once filled the hole I had noticed and we would slice into them with a wood-handled bread knife all summer long, cutting off and throwing away the first slice because the flies had usually had a go at the salami. They were delicious.

The cooking area of the kitchen at Port an Droighionn is at one end of the room and the dining table at the other; the smells from the North African lamb filled the room and Jane, Dominic and I ate it with chunks of bread and a salad, dipping the bread into the unused salt and gazing out at our bay and at the eight miles of sea and the islands on the horizon.

'Who needs television when you have this?' my mother used to say as she sat looking out at the view from this table, after she had finished cooking for us and had come to eat. We would gnaw her rosemary-covered lamb chops to the bone. There was always something new to watch from that window – some sudden shaft of sunlight tearing through the clouds and splashing on to the leaden sea, or a gannet plummeting vertically into the water, or a seal poking his head out from the bay and staring up at the house with his dark, round eyes.

The next morning, after breakfast, my sister and I walked

down the slope, and a minute later we were standing in our Wellington boots in the sea. Our mother's will, the simplest of documents, made out on a form bought from a stationer's, explained that she wished her ashes to be scattered into the sea at Port an Droighionn. There was barely a breeze, which was helpful. I didn't want bits of her on my clothes. Together, we held the plastic urn and tipped its contents into the clear water, the small, eddying waves taking the cloud of ashes out into the ocean. I dunked the urn into the water to rinse it out, and my sister and I put our arms around each other.

In the late afternoon I stood down by the shore for a long time, looking at the sky, which was changing every second as the sun tumbled red into the sea where the islands floated on the horizon. My mother had sat on those rocks, telling me stories of the mermaids and mermen who swam around under the waves we were looking at. We had lain on our backs nearby and pointed to the shapes we saw in the clouds.

'I know this sounds odd,' I said to my sister when I came back up to the house before dinner, 'but I've worked out where Mum is. For me, at least. She's literally in the sea and in the sky.'

'OK,' my sister said. 'I see.'

'I feel I can talk to her that way. I'll be able to visit her and talk to her in the sky and the sea. I feel better.'

Only, days later, I knew I had been conning myself. My mother remained nowhere to me. She was just gone.

I decided we needed a memorial stone to her. That would give me a focal point for my grief, some way to bring her back, somewhere to talk to her. People go to graves to talk to the dead, don't they?

Weeks and months passed. I found an engraver. I went back to Port an Droighionn and looked for the right stone. I picked some up. Turned others over to see how flat they were. I left them all on the shore and walked back to the house. I was conning myself once more.

She was nowhere. She was just gone.

9

I had, at least, some relics.

I now kept many of my clothes in my mother's dark, antique tall boy. Its drawers reeked of my mother's clothes, which reeked of the tens of thousands of cigarettes she had smoked while wearing the clothes. My clean sweaters came out smelling as if I had worked a night shift with chain-smoking mortuary workers. I loved that smell and longed for it to stay.

I set up my parents' old kitchen table – oak, classically English, painted black but sanded down in sections by my father thirty years earlier, a single Chiquita banana sticker pressed to its underside by me or my sister around the same time – in my study and it became my desk.

Over the dining table loomed my severe, unsmiling, black-lace-wearing maternal great-great-grandmother, painted by her husband, a well-known Scottish painter of the nineteenth century. My mother, perhaps eighteen years old and wearing a yellow shirt and blue sweater, now smiled gently from my study wall in a portrait I had never before seen, had never known about. Prints I had gazed at for hours as a child and had entirely forgotten – William Blake's etching of Chaucer's pilgrims; country gentlemen in top hats examining a salmon just fished out of a river – emerged from my sister's attic, where so many of my itinerant mother's possessions had remained hidden for years until Jane and I began sorting through them in the months after her death. I took her glasses and their case and found a single grey hair snagged in the nose rests; I put it carefully into a round brass box with a lid and clasp.

During the summer and autumn of 2005 we worked our way through a hundred boxes of linen tablecloths, coffee-stained mugs, wooden eggcups, Middle Eastern cushions, pillowcases and, most precious to me, battered kitchen implements. I picked out a potato masher and big serving spoons and two spatulas and two Sabatier knives whose blades had been sharpened over forty years into slightly wavy lines; a blue Le Creuset oval casserole dish; terracotta tapas dishes; a dark-green tureen; a dozen small brown cauldron-shaped ceramic pots. As many relics of her kitchens as I could fit into my kitchen drawers and on shelves. These things had been used, not just looked at. And I remembered their being used. I had benefited from their use, over and over again. They introduced me to a thousand sources of joy: chocolate mousse, roast chicken, steak. You wouldn't have been able to sell them at a car boot sale, but to me they were invaluable.

We were in no hurry to sort through it all. We did it in bursts. I wanted to string this out as long as possible, this rediscovery of my mother's possessions – and my mother – with my sister, whose memories were sharper and broader than mine. She had always welcomed family lore when I had shrugged it off, hostile to a past that seemed to hold nothing but sadness. Memories tripped out of her as we sorted through the piles. I began to see the past, for the first time, as something I might be able to cherish rather than flee from.

'She bought you this as a wedding present,' my sister said, as we gazed at an entire Wedgwood dinner service. It had a green and gold trim that wasn't exactly ugly but wasn't exactly to my taste. I had been a teenager or perhaps in my early twenties when our mother bought this, Jane explained. We laughed briefly, both of us knowing without having to say anything how many of our mother's impulses went into buying it: sweet preparation for her son's future marital home; anachronistic grandiosity in buying something so formal; wasteful extravagance from a woman who at one point spent her nights in youth hostels while utterly convinced that she had the resources of a Russian princess. It was a shallow sort of laughter.

I was anxious about Christmas. There was quite a potential for tears. It was our first without our mother. My father's partner, Molly, had recently lost her beloved son Rafe, an aid worker, killed by an anti-tank mine in Darfur. And my girlfriend's father, who lived in Vancouver, had cancer that was resisting treatment. But there was an upside: with our mother dead, we could spend Christmas with our father for the first time in many years, at his and Molly's beautiful, cosy stone house, hidden in the folds of the Perthshire hills. And Molly's cooking was guaranteed to be extraordinary.

My girlfriend, Jane and I took the train north – with presents overhead rather than our mother's ashes – and were deluged with warmth when we arrived.

'What can I get you to drink?' my father said, almost as soon as we were inside, the coal stove filling the open-plan living room and kitchen with heat.

'Are you hungry?' Molly asked.

No one talked about death. No one cried.

On Boxing Day Jane, my girlfriend and I walked through the fog that lay heavy over Perthshire and climbed a nearby hill. When we reached the top the fog broke briefly to give us a view down to the house and beyond.

As we walked down the hill I remembered moments of Christmases past. My mother taking offence at the seating plan at my grandmother's dining table and announcing: 'Don, get the children ready, we're leaving.' My father's phone ringing on Christmas morning: 'OK, we'll come and get you. Hang on! Mum's thrown Jane out and she's on the pavement outside the house.' My mother showing up drunk and ranting in my grandparents' living room, staggering around in front of the delicate porcelain figures of sword fighters that stood at the end of the room on a shelf. My mother – drunk, Christmas after Christmas. I missed her terribly.

On an afternoon in January, months after the process of dividing up the spoils of death had begun, Jane and I sat on the floor of her living room going through the last of our mother's things.

Family diamonds and pearl brooches were laid out messily in a tan jewel case; some photographs of a beautiful young woman in the mid-1960s, posing for her photographer husband, my father; CDs that I had given her and was now taking back. All that was left to divide up between us now were her books. We each kept some art books, some novels, some poetry, some history. We put others aside for the charity shop. My sister took the gardening books. I didn't care much about flowers and vegetables.

'Can I have the cookery books, then?' I asked my sister.

'Sure, but can I keep *French Country Cooking*?' she said. 'It was Elizabeth David's first book.' And therefore, we both understood, our mother's most precious cookery book.

As my sister pushed the gardening books towards her side of the room, I picked up *A Book of Mediterranean Food* from the pile of cookery books sitting on the beige carpet. My sister, I realized some weeks later, was wrong about *French Country Cooking*. *A Book of Mediterranean Food* was, in fact, Elizabeth David's first book, published in 1950 during the years of postwar rationing. My mother's copy, worn and yellow, was a reissue that had appeared in 1965. A Penguin Handbook, it's called, and a handbook is what it is. A revolutionary instruction manual for a generation of women who had very little idea how to cook. Years before Julia Child, decades before Jamie Oliver. It was a book of joy emerging from a continent that still staggered from six years of war, of evil and death and scarcity. The war is over, it seemed to be saying to women at the time, and now it is time to celebrate around the table together, to smell, to taste, to drink, to feast. I flicked through it. I picked up *The Robert Carrier Cookbook*. Who ever talked about Robert Carrier now? But in our home, he had been like an unseen member of the family. My mother's careful rectangles of tape kept the thing hanging together. Drops of something brown – early versions of sauce for spare ribs? – spattered pages 336 and 337, the latter of which featured the recipe we used to love. I had forgotten about spare ribs.

Katie Stewart was another happy spirit in our house. I took up the disintegrating copy of *The Times Cookery Book* – just referred to as 'Katie Stewart' by my mother – and I remembered that this book had furnished me with the recipe I had chosen for my first ever attempt, at age sixteen, at cooking for girls in the hope they might have sex with me. 'Chicory with Ham in Cheese Sauce', pages 57 to 59. It was not good and it did not work. In the pile was a beautiful 1909 copy of *Mrs Beeton's Family Cookery* and the sensible-looking two-volume *Good Housekeeping Cookery Encyclopedia*.

And there were the Elizabeth Davids, the books my mother had in recent years implored me to read, telling me over and over again that if I wanted to learn how to cook I could find out how through Elizabeth David. I had ignored her advice while she was alive. I'd glanced at the books – largely unillustrated, page after page of writing. Recipes by an old lady, they looked like. Time-consuming textbooks rather than easy-to-read cookery books. I preferred the warmth and pictures and hand-holding of the matey Jamie Oliver and the impossibly tricksy vertical food of three-star New York chefs.

'I couldn't make a piece of toast when I married your father,' my mother had told me. 'Elizabeth David taught me everything.' These were the books that led her lovingly, excitedly, beyond toast. *French Country Cooking. Italian Food. Spices, Salt and Aromatics in the English Kitchen. An Omelette and a Glass of Wine.*

My mother was not in the first generation of women to have their eyes opened by Elizabeth David to olive oil, garlic and olives. She was seven when, in 1950, the young Elizabeth David put together a collection of recipes she had picked up during her travels around the Mediterranean before, during and after the war. That book was considered by many to be horribly presumptuous: where, exactly, was a British house-wife meant to find an aubergine, whatever that was, in a country still under the strictures of rationing? But to many others the book was a thrill, an escape to an exotic, delicious world. My aunt Kata told me that reading Elizabeth David's books felt like reading a good novel. And in time, partly thanks to her efforts and her books, the Mediterranean did start to come to Britain in the shape of imported Parma ham, mozza-rella, unusual vegetables like courgettes, fresh herbs and olive oil that wasn't only available in chemists for earache. Luckily for my mother, the revolution Elizabeth David helped start in British shops and restaurants was well under way by the 1960s, so she could do more than just dream of Mediterranean food.

There was one final book in the pile. It had a dirtied blue leather cover and gold lower-case lettering that said, simply, 'cookery book'. I opened it, glanced at the yellowed newspaper clippings and the handwritten recipes in a jagged, peaked script I knew as well as my own. I was shocked at how much life there could be in a dead person's handwriting. I closed it quickly.

I knew in that moment that there was one way I might bring my mother back: heading to the kitchen and cooking her recipes. Her spare ribs, her chocolate crispies, her straw-berry ice cream – they could be my portals to a past I barely remembered, a past I'd willed myself to forget. Food is one of the great memory-joggers. Conjuring certain tastes, combining certain flavours together in the kitchen, could perhaps whisk me back to a time when I sat on a wooden stool next to the stove and watched my mother sweep her spatula around a mixing bowl, happily leaving traces of melted chocolate that could be collected only by my finger. Even though she was dead, I could share with her something that bound us and our whole family together in the good years. In the kitchen, any kitchen, I had always felt close to having a family, even when all four constituent parts of that family were living in different houses in different countries, tension and anger and silence separating us. Over a chopping board with a sharp knife in my hand, something bubbling on the stove nearby, a glass of wine on the worktop, I felt part of something good, something loving – even if I was in Jerusalem or Baghdad. Ever since it disintegrated, I had missed my own family and felt drawn to the tables of other people's families. And I had longed to build a family of my own, a family that could sit around a table and eat and talk and laugh.

I wanted to put back together what had long ago been lost and broken.

My mother could help me with that, I decided. She could help me drag her back from the past so that I could almost feel her with me, in the kitchen. I was sure of it. I should read her cookery books. I should do as she'd told me over and over again – read and learn from Elizabeth David. And I should keep learning until I no longer needed to keep the books open on my kitchen table as I made her food. Then, presumably, I would be able to cook – as she defined it. More than paintings and tablecloths, these books and her recipes might open up my closed memory so that I could bring back the young, sane, beautiful mother of whom I had only fragmented memories. My mother had not looked after me for about twenty-five years. I wanted back the woman I had known for the first ten years of my life, the woman who placed heavenly, delicious food at the centre of our family and of my relationship with her. She had read these pages and learned from Elizabeth David, her mind opening to Elizabeth David's revolutionizing evocation of the Mediterranean world of garlic, olive oil, wine and

48

French quayside restaurants. My mother had made this food and taken joy from feeding people she loved. She had turned her kitchen into a magnet for her family. I couldn't call her up and ask for cooking advice any more, but perhaps I didn't need to; her books could teach me everything she had known.

Breakfast at Port an Droighionn

10

The famous cookery writer Elizabeth David has, with friends who are more business-minded than she, opened a shop named Elizabeth David Ltd. It is on a street behind Sloane Square, and it has become a temple for people interested in food. It is 1965 and Elizabeth David is now a slightly fetishized figure in Britain. She and her friends realize that a kitchen shop selling utensils, pots, pans and dishes sourced by her and sold by her could prove enormously profitable. Her writing in books, newspapers and magazines has unparalleled influence in the British food world and beyond. She complains to a man from the Le Creuset kitchenware company that she is bored with their yellow-coloured enamelware and wants to see blue casserole dishes, gratin dishes, pots and pans. Blue like the colour of the packets of Gauloises she smokes. Two years later the company obliges, and in 1967 she is the first to sell blue Le Creuset in Britain.

The shop becomes Elizabeth David's realm, more important to her for several years than her writing. People come for advice, for guidance, for a glance at her. The famous send notes or stop by, many of them friends – Peggy Guggenheim, Freya Stark, Princess Margaret and Lord Snowdon, Len Deighton, Robert Carrier and the woman who was in many ways Elizabeth David's successor, Jane Grigson, who dies before her mentor and whose food my father often photographs for the *Observer*'s Sunday magazine. Elizabeth David eats there, drinks there, socializes there, holds court there.

My mother is drawn, like thousands, to 46 Bourne Street.

She enters the shop with my father one beautifully sunny Saturday morning in the late 1960s. The window display, by the designer Anthony Denney, is unlike anything my mother has ever seen. On the wooden table in the window is a symmetrical, interwoven, almost sculpted pile of pots, pans and utensils. Around her are blue-grey walls with white shelves full of French and English kitchen equipment – soufflé dishes, cast-iron frying pans and glowing yellow and orange Le Creuset casserole dishes, whose lids are surprisingly, reassuringly heavy. The tiles on the floor are black and white, and they, too, are covered in pots and pans and roasting tins, stacked, almost overflowing, and slightly overwhelming to my mother. She has never seen anything like this. No one in Britain has. It's like walking into the fantasy kitchen that Elizabeth David's books have conjured up over the past fifteen years for a generation of people, mainly women, who were still making do with post-war rations when the first book was published.

Down the narrow stairs in the basement, where the owner has her cubby-hole office – she likes to drink wine in there and brings in lunch for the friends she hires to work in the shop – is another room full of items that Elizabeth David has personally hunted down on long journeys through the back roads of France and England. My mother and father walk down the steps, and there is Elizabeth David herself deep in conversation with a man – about food, of course. Some other customers, supplicants, wait in line for the word. My mother does not talk to her. My father finds her formidable.

Elizabeth David has already published most of her great cookery books. She has lived in Greece, Egypt, India and Italy. She has been married and divorced and disappointed in love many times. In 1963, she suffered a cerebral haemorrhage that wiped out two arenas of passion: she can no longer taste salt and she is no longer much interested in sex. The shop is her new love.

My mother is piecing together her kitchen. She is in her mid-twenties, thirty years younger than Elizabeth David, building her home, her family, her kitchen. This is the first of many visits to the shop, and my mother is following its owner's advice: 'Some sensible person once remarked that you spend the whole of your life either in your bed or your shoes', Elizabeth David writes in *French Country Cooking*, which my mother has read from cover to cover. 'Having done the best you can by shoes and bed, devote all the time and resources at your disposal to the building up of a fine kitchen. It will be, as it should be, the most comforting and comfortable room in the house.'

My mother's kitchen in the house on Elizabeth Close is tiny. There's no room in it for cookery books, so my mother has to cross the small landing to pick them off a shelf in the living room if she needs to consult Elizabeth David or the others in her growing collection. The address, in Little Venice, is fashionable, but the house my father's father has helped pay for as a wedding gift is narrow, and soon they will move to a bigger place nearby on Ashworth Road. In the meantime, my mother crams ever more into the pale-blue cabinets that line the kitchen's walls. There's a blue Le Creuset gratin dish from Elizabeth David Ltd; a set of industrial-sized aluminium pots and pans that are a gift from her mother, who owns a hotel in Edinburgh and has access to restaurant suppliers; earthenware dishes found in a market in Puerto Pollensa in Majorca, where her father often docks his yacht, *Xanadu*.

Many of the pots and pans in my mother's kitchen come from the shoots my father does for advertisements, magazines and books in his studio near Chancery Lane. He takes a lot of pictures of food, and those photographs require props – knives, wooden spoons, serving platters, jugs, storage jars, casserole dishes, a large salt jar. Some can be reused in later shots, but eventually many of them make their way back to our house.

Food comes too. To get one perfect chicken for an ad or the illustration of a Jane Grigson recipe in the *Observer* magazine, my father and his assistants will buy ten. Not all of them will be cooked during the day, so the uncooked chickens, sirloins, lamb chops, and the bags of carrots, lettuce, fruit, cakes often end up with us.

My mother's younger sister, Kata, is also learning to cook, but she's spending a year at the Constance Spry school in central London, learning first flower arranging and then cooking. She is dyslexic. University, in these days, isn't an option for her. She's only sixteen or seventeen, and her parents have sent her to live in a convent in Hampstead – 'a good, safe place for a virgin to live,' she calls it later in life – where she shares a room with a granddaughter of the King of Belgium. When she can, she escapes, walking down the broad, busy Finchley Road to my parents' house and my mother's little kitchen.

It's lunchtime, and Kata sits down at the table next to the window that looks out on to the local pub. My mother reaches into the oven and takes out two small ceramic cauldron-shaped brown ramekins known as cocottes. They have been sitting in a shallow pan of boiling water for a few minutes with the lid on. Inside the little dishes are 'Les Oeufs en Cocotte à la Crème' from *French Provincial Cooking*, Elizabeth David's fifth and most popular book, a 500-page exploration of French food that gives Elizabeth David's American friend, Julia Child, anxious hours because it comes out two years before her *Mastering the Art of French Cooking*. My mother, many years later, gives a copy of *French Provincial Cooking* to my sister. The inscription reads: 'The Bible! Happy Cooking!'

The egg dish is not light. There are three ingredients: eggs, butter and cream. The butter melts in each pot, the eggs follow, and when they begin to harden, the cream goes on top. Elizabeth David writes: 'This is one of the most delicious egg dishes ever invented, but it is rare to get it properly done.'

Kata spoons her egg out of the cocotte. There is also some pâté spread on toast. It is a delicious, simple combination. My mother makes the recipe one of her regular Elizabeth David dishes.

☙

Les Oeufs en Cocotte à la Crème

You need ramekins for this. Or the little cauldron-like ceramic dishes that are also great for small, individualized desserts like *petits pots de crème*.

Heat the oven or boil some water in a wide pan. Put a little butter inside each ramekin and then place the ramekins in the shallow water or in the oven so that the butter melts. Break an egg into each ramekin and then cover. When the eggs are nearly done – it only takes two or three minutes – pour some double cream on top of each one. Take them out soon after and be generous with the salt and pepper before tucking in. Toast is good to have nearby. If you really love someone, bring them this in bed on a Saturday morning. On a tray with freshly squeezed orange juice, a thick slice of toast and a bowl of *café au lait*.

11

There was one major problem with my plan to spend hours in the kitchen, hours reading cookery books. I was a foreign correspondent. I did not have a domesticated lifestyle. 'You need to know,' I had told the woman who would later become my wife when we began to date seriously, 'that this is the only thing I know how to do. It's the only way I can make money. Besides, I love it. I will never stop doing it. I will always travel. I will always be away for much of the year.'

'Sure,' she said, 'that's fine. I'm busy too, you know.'

She meant it, too; she truly didn't mind my going away for long spells. But I minded, more and more.

The truth was, I had begun, for some indistinct period of months or possibly a couple of years, to feel less in love with war zones than I proclaimed.

This was me at thirty: I was with my dear friend Richard Miron, a radio reporter for the BBC, and we were making our way through a dusty lemon grove in the Gaza Strip at the start of the Second Intifada. It was the autumn of 2000. We were near a heavily fortified Israeli army position, and in recent days the Israeli soldiers, unseen behind their walls of concrete, had been shooting dead quite a few Palestinians. The lemon trees provided us with cover, but then the bullets started zipping through the heavy early-afternoon citrus air of Gaza and past us, breaking the sound barrier in a sharp crack. 'Look at these lemons,' I said, stopping to pick some off a tree as we ran through the grove with our bodies bent low. 'They're the most lemony lemons I've ever smelled.'

'What the fuck are you doing?' Richard said.

'Picking fruit,' I replied, stuffing the firm lemons and their green pointy leaves into my pockets. I tore one open, and the sour, delicious juice dripped down my hand. The perfect meeting of a fresh ingredient with a life-threatening moment. I was very happy. 'They can't see us among all these trees, you know.' The bullets continued to crack nearby.

Something would happen in my brain in those moments. The fight-or-flight chemical, norepinephrine, seemed to surge inside me, making me feel hyper-alert, almost limitlessly strong and completely in control of my body. I experienced a beatific calm, a sense of extraordinary well-being and generosity. The lemons glowed with the deepest yellow. Their leaves seemed perfectly formed. My friend Richard was the most amiable companion possible. A distilled form of friendship was born amid the flying lead and the norepinephrine. Richard would be a friend for life, I immediately knew. I wanted to stay in the grove all afternoon gathering these perfect lemons with my friend.

'This is ridiculous. I'm getting the fuck out of here,' he said, turning his back on me. I followed.

This was me at thirty-six about a year after my mother died and at the end of years of visiting and living in war zones: slumped against the wall of the Jabal Amel Hospital in the southern Lebanese city of Tyre, I tried to get a Lebanese man's blood off the soles of my sneakers and on to the pavement. I looked at the sky where the unseen Israeli drones were buzzing and began to think about a meal I would cook when I got home. I needed to start on my Elizabeth David-led course of self-education. It would be from my copy of *French Country Cooking*, which I kept in my bag at all times during this bad, stupid war. It would be a heavy meal, aggressively extravagant, with bacon-fatty casseroles, tureens of soup with potatoes, desserts with cream, so much warm heaviness that my guests would be pinned down by the weight and the homeliness and the cosiness of a classic French meal.

There was not a lot of conversation going on right now as my friends and I sat and stood outside the hospital. A photographer friend pulled on a cigarette and said, 'This is the last one, honestly. I'm not doing any more wars.'

'Same,' I said. We both knew we were lying, and yet I recognized the trapped look in his face. How else could he make a living? How else could I? Wouldn't we miss it too much?

We had just come out of the emergency department of Jabal Amel. It had become the main stage in the most pointless and one of the most vicious wars I had ever covered. This was where the medics, themselves targets for Israeli missiles, brought the injured.

Inside, moments earlier, we had watched a man die. We had tried to avoid slipping on his blood, which had poured on to the square tiles of the hospital floor when the porters had carried him into the room. By then he had only one arm attached to his body, and his instantly barbecued flesh was filling the room with a bitter meat smell. The doctors had not really bothered. They had placed a transparent plastic tube down his throat, but it was a token gesture. After about a minute he was dead. One of the doctors, his hands protected by white latex gloves, had felt around in the exposed mess of muscle and windpipe and blood and spine in the man's neck and had pulled out a two-inch piece of metal. It was one of many pieces of the three Israeli rockets that had sliced into the man as he stood with a small cup of coffee in his hand on the side of the road a few minutes earlier.

'Ah,' the doctor had said, holding up the rocket fragment for the others to see.

My friends and I milled about outside. We were all suddenly desperately thirsty and drank all the water we could find.

I saw these friends in places like this, places like Tyre, in the middle of wars that subsided and then elided into more wars, mainly those that were the ever-growing concentric ripples caused by the events of 11 September 2001. Some of them had been at my wedding a few months earlier. We had been very close to this attack, rushing down the road towards the targeted Lebanese man after the first two missiles hit him, not anticipating the third. Three of our group had come back from the scene with their own minor wounds. I thought back to the cocktail of super-human energy and Zen calm I had felt in the lemon grove in Gaza, the hills of Kosovo, the streets of Nablus in the West Bank, at times even in the middle of the battle of Fallujah. That feeling was gone. Now I just wanted to get away. Fight had been worn down to raw flight. I knew war and its set pieces well: suicide bombings, roadside bombs, sniper bullets.

The novelty of horror makes it attractive. The sense that recording that horror might help to end it is also a powerful draw. And then there are those delicious, addictive chemicals in the brain.

But when it all becomes too familiar, when the almost out-of-body experiences dry up, and when your increasingly ineffectual words are buried on page thirty-something of the newspaper on day thirty-something of a war between irrational actors who couldn't care less what journalists from the United States write about, well, then there is less of a reason to stay. And when the danger level is as high as it was in southern Lebanon, it becomes even harder to understand why you are still there. I had stayed in the south of the country, where it was most dangerous, and I had made a mistake. But by then we were stuck in Tyre, unable to travel safely.

I hid in the imaginings of unexplored culinary lands, places of comfort where I knew I could not do much good to the world at large, but perhaps I could make my friends and family happy. And myself.

'I've never made pastry,' I thought. 'That would be new and challenging. I've never boiled potatoes for gnocchi, boned a duck, prised open oysters or cooked a soufflé. I've never made cassoulet. I should definitely make a cassoulet when I get home.'

When the afternoon at the hospital was over, I lay on my bed, and the warm summer Mediterranean wind passed through the open windows of the white apartment in the old city of Tyre. I was renting the apartment from an old man who had refused to leave town. The breeze licked at the pages of *French Country Cooking*. I hoped Elizabeth David would relax me, but instead she began to put me a little on edge. Her prose scared me. She was bossy. I was not used to this – contemporary cookery book writers want to be your friend (Jamie), your lover (Nigella) or your mentor (Batali; Jean-Georges).

I was also rather taken aback at the tone because I happened to have just seen a wonderful BBC film about Elizabeth David called *Elizabeth David: A Life in Recipes*, in which the most attractive Mrs David seemed to be a lot of fun. She was in and out of bed with various men, drank copiously and seemed altogether very badly behaved. I had expected her to seduce me through her books, not to tell me off.

But then I read this: 'I should be surprised to hear that anybody had ever followed any cookery book menu in every detail.' This was news to me. Recipes and instructions, I thought, were written in books for a simple reason – because they were correct, perfect, precise. Apparently it wasn't quite as simple as that.

As I read more of her recipes, I noticed something else that seemed both reassuring and alarming: Elizabeth David doesn't always tell you exactly what to do. Most modern cookery books lead you by the hand. Frequently, Elizabeth David doesn't give precise measurements or cooking times or temperatures.

And yet she can be quite the rigid, rule-issuing school-mistress. She discusses, for example, what 'sole cooked in a rich sauce of cream and mushrooms' might go with: 'It must not be preceded by a creamy mushroom soup, nor followed by chicken cooked in a cream sauce. Have some regard for the digestions of others even if your own resembles that of the ostrich.'

Her voice seemed familiar to me somehow: authoritarian, but interested in devolving power, not hoarding it. She knows that she knows best, but she wants to pass on her knowledge and she wants you to try and fail until you have worked it out for yourself.

I wondered whether my mother liked Mrs David's blend of imperiousness and passionate enthusiasm so much because it matched her own. Or was it the other way round and she had learned it partly from Elizabeth David?

I thought of my precious kitchen table at home in London – the table my mother had cooked on, which was of no value to anyone but Jane and me. In 1994, two years after her death, the contents of Elizabeth David's kitchen were auctioned off in a frenzy of bidding at Phillips. Hundreds of people showed up, desperately bidding for a wooden spoon, a casserole dish, a whisk, a spatula. Some people did not even know what they had purchased after their frenzied bids. It didn't matter, as long as Mrs David had used it in her kitchen. 'Sacred relics,' Clarissa Dickson Wright calls them when she describes the auction in her introduction to a later edition of *A Book of Mediterranean Food*. Prue Leith, the writer, restaurateur and cookery teacher, won the bidding for Elizabeth David's famous kitchen table, on which she both cooked and wrote. 'I'm going to cook on it just like she did, and think of her,' she said. 'She was the most important cookery writer this century.'

As I read and learned about Elizabeth David I noticed some small parallels between her life and my mother's, even though Elizabeth David was three decades older. They both had a dash of South-East Asian blood – Sumatran in the case of Elizabeth David, Burmese in the case of my mother. They both spent time on Malta; both went to finishing schools in Europe. They both drank; both veered precariously between being fearsome and enormously warm; both had health problems; both divorced and both remained unmarried at death.

I sat up in my bed and looked out at the Mediterranean, which both my mother and Elizabeth David had adored. 'Many of us would do well to *mediterraneanize* ourselves for a season, to quicken those ethnic roots from which has sprung so much of what is best in our nature,' advised Norman Douglas, who became Elizabeth David's great teacher of Mediterranean food and life. I agreed but I suspect being stuck in a beseiged Lebanese city wasn't what Douglas had in mind.

There was so little to eat in the cut-off city by this stage of the war that on some days we had to rely on the local fishermen who swam out beyond the reefs and past the rip current to throw dynamite into the waves, collecting the stunned fish as they floated to the surface. The fishermen knew that Israeli missiles would sink them if they got into their boats.

The men explained that the dynamiting was an old technique, not limited to times of siege – and not always successful. Or safe. One young man walked around with stumps at the end of his arms.

One evening, the fishermen we befriended set out a long table on the rocks between the crashing water and the old city walls. At the appointed time we threaded our way barefoot through the narrow, ancient streets to pick at the bombed fish they had grilled for us. The white flesh was delicious and tender. We brought the beer, and together we drank it and filled the warm night with laughter. We stripped to our underwear and swam in the black sea while unseen Israeli helicopters thwacked away at the sky somewhere overhead. These nightly, threatening vespers scared us because we knew they could see us. I myself had looked down on human targets from the user end of that technology once before. Standing with a group of American soldiers gathered in a tent in Iraq, I had watched a green-tinged computer-screen image fed from a drone over Fallujah as they guided a bomb on to a house of insurgents. We could clearly see each man until the bomb hit. But even if the Israelis were watching us now from a command centre in Tel Aviv, as I had watched the Iraqi insurgents, we were not to be deterred. We laughed and swam. It felt, for an evening, as if we had escaped. We were friends around a table filled with fish and beer.

It was time for me to scale back my visits to war zones. I had my mother's Elizabeth David books to guide me to something else. It was time to celebrate around a table, to smell, to taste, to drink, to feast. And I now had someone to do that with. A wife.

12

I had met a girl one evening in a friend's apartment in Little Venice. It was at the end of 2003 and I had just moved to London. We sat next to each other at dinner, and I twirled her around later when someone put some old standards on the stereo.

Her name was Pernilla. It took me two or three times to get the name right. By the time I had it right, I realized that the woman who bore it had the most amazing ability to make me happy. So we went to Rome for New Year.

At about a quarter to midnight on 31 December, I felt a sharp pain in my left side. We were on the second or third course of a seven-course *prix fixe* menu in a romantic spot near the Via Condotti. I felt the embarrassment of someone who is about to get very ill at a very inconvenient moment. It worsened. I was about to ruin our first big, romantic trip together.

'You know, I hate to say this, but I have an incredibly sharp pain in my side,' I told Pernilla.

I took some breaths and a sip of wine and it went completely away.

At five minutes to midnight, Pernilla looked at me and said: 'This is odd, but now I have a pain in my left side.'

She took some breaths and a sip of wine, but her pain did not go away. Just after midnight, as everyone in the restaurant settled down to course number four after shaking hands and kissing their fellow diners, we left. I dragged Pernilla through the packed streets, and I could see that everyone who passed by thought she was very drunk. There were no taxis. I walked her across a bridge over the cold Tiber and we reached the hotel. She was very ill, vomiting from the pain.

The following day, still in pain, Pernilla insisted on going to the Sistine Chapel.

'I don't think that's a good idea,' I said. 'You're really not well.'

'But we're in Rome. We can't just stay in this hotel room.'

It was raining outside, and cold. We stood in the queue to get into the Vatican Museum for ten minutes.

'This is ridiculous,' I said. 'You can't stand here in the rain.'

'OK, but let's go to the Baths of Caracalla. Promise me. We're in Rome!'

We got a taxi and Pernilla staggered round the red-brick ruins of the Roman baths, wincing with pain.

'OK, enough? Can I take you back to the hotel now?' I asked.

'Can we go shopping? Please.'

We went to Alberta Ferretti and Pernilla tried on a beautiful black dress. 'You've got ink all over your chin, you know,' I told her quietly, when she came out of the changing room.

Pernilla looked in a mirror. 'No, I'm just cold,' she said.

'That's not good,' I said. 'You are blue. Really blue.'

She got worse. Eventually, on our third night in the hotel, I asked the concierge for directions to the nearest hospital casualty department. Three hospitals and an ambulance later, we made a break for the airport. I worship Italy. I think it is God's gift to the world, especially its food. But I have seen better-equipped hospitals in Afghanistan than the ones Pernilla saw in Rome.

'Could you bring some toilet paper?' Pernilla said, calling me from the third hospital she was taken to. They told her she had a kidney stone and they would operate in a couple of days, after their saint's day holiday. They were wrong – her kidney was failing – and we sensed the situation was more serious than they thought it was. She was exhausted. We didn't speak Italian and none of the medical staff spoke more than a few words of English.

'Do you know what they gave me for lunch?' Pernilla asked me. 'Spaghetti with ketchup. This is Italy and they gave me spaghetti with ketchup. I want to go home.' I called the airline and bought new tickets, for that afternoon.

We did not tell the doctors we were leaving. They must have returned from their holiday to find an empty room.

That's how Pernilla began what we grew to call her special weight-loss programme. First went a failed kidney, the source of the incredible pain in Rome. Weeks later, they wheeled her away from me on a bed in a hospital in west London.

'Bye, see you soon,' she said, smiling as if to cheer me up.

Over the months I had now spent with Pernilla, I had discovered that she had an unusual amount of energy. Late at night, just before bed, she often had a bit of a boogie – music not required – in the bedroom. There was a disco in her head. And first thing in the morning, as I lay groggy and barely conscious, she would often bounce on me, laughing, her long hair in my face, tickling it. 'You're a total Tigger,' I said. The morning bouncings came to be known as Tiggerings.

In the hospital shop I looked for a cuddly Tigger but they only had Pooh and Piglet. I bought her a Piglet. 'Piglet just worries about everything,' Pernilla said when she woke up after the operation. 'I think you needed someone to worry with.'

Over the next weeks and months, a few other bits and pieces had to come out of Pernilla's body. There were tests, bad-looking shapes appearing on scans, fresh surgeons for each new region of her body. And still she managed to make me happier than anyone I had known. She took me to wonderful exhibitions I wouldn't have gone to; a Sigmar Polke show at Tate Britain I enjoyed hating because of his trite treatment of the war in Afghanistan; the Cast Collection at the Victoria and Albert, a room packed with plaster casts of the ancient world's greatest hits. She took me to the Barbican to see *The Black Rider*, an avante-garde opera so awful that I couldn't sleep through it. She took me to a Swedish Christmas carol service in St Paul's, so entrancing that the packed cathedral, between hymns, was completely silent. She had grown up in Vancouver riding horses and, on a holiday in Ecuador, she got me on a horse called Palomino. I had barely cantered before but within three minutes of climbing aboard Palomino – Western saddle, no helmet, just a cowboy hat – we were galloping into the Andes. 'I'm going to die any second,' I thought to myself, as Palomino took off after Pernilla and our guide, José, and then, 'Fuck it. I always wanted to be Steve McQueen.' And I tapped Palomino with my heels and, apparently delighted to have someone of his own mind-set on top of him, he galloped even faster. I felt as though I was floating. We rode through the mountains for seven hours, along narrow paths and through rivers in the forest. Pernilla rode in front of me, often turning round in her saddle to check if I was OK, meeting my grin with one of her own. Somewhere in the Andes I realized that Pernilla was, unconsciously, teaching me a lesson by example: not every thrilling experience on the planet involved guns, bombs and killing. She leaped on to horses she had never ridden with the speed at which I had once run towards buses in Jerusalem that had just blown up.

I first told her I was in love with her in February 2004, while sitting in a chilly winter garden in Baghdad. Everyone else in the house I was renting a room in was asleep, including, dismayingly, the Iraqi guard who my friend Adam, the landlord, had hired to monitor the closed circuit TV screens that sat on a ledge by the front door. I called Pernilla on my satellite phone. She was walking through a park in London. 'Also,' I said, apropos of nothing I had just said, 'I just wanted to tell you that I love you.' There was silence on the end of the line and she didn't say it back but she seemed, I thought, pleased. She said she had just had to sit down on a bench.

A year later I was back in Baghdad, sitting in my hotel room one afternoon, when a bullet ricocheted around my balcony. A hot, twisted slug ended up on the white tiles, next to the white plastic picnic table I sometimes sat at to get what passed for fresh air in Baghdad. I assumed it was just a random round fired from a rifle that had arced through the sky of Baghdad from a mile or two away, perhaps fired into the sky in celebration of a wedding. It wasn't personal.

But that bullet seemed like a quiet sign to me that Iraq was not my place any longer. I left two days later. I had decided to ask Pernilla to marry me when I got back.

A few days after returning from Iraq, on a Saturday afternoon in February 2005, I took her out for lunch at the restaurant where we had gone on our first date. Then we walked up to the top of Primrose Hill in the hoary cold. We had spent quite a long time kissing on top of the hill on our second date.

We bumped into a friend of mine on the way up the hill. I was feeling a little nauseous and was terse with my friend and yanked Pernilla away quickly, climbing the hill with a hardened purpose.

At the top I held her in my arms and asked her to marry me.

'You should take your time and think about it a bit,' I said.

'That's OK, I can make up my mind up now,' she said. 'Yes.'

'Are you sure because you can think about it a bit, you know. I travel a lot. I think you should take some time to think about it.'

'No, really, it's OK. I can answer now. Yes.'

'Oh, OK.'

I was now signed up to spend the rest of my life with another human being. I was slightly freaked out. Pernilla's nose was rosy in the cold. A dog ran past. I put my hand into my jacket pocket.

'Then I have something for you,' I said, and I took out a small box from my pocket and gave Pernilla my grandmother's engagement ring.

We walked to the nearest pub and drank glasses of champagne in a corner, not quite believing what we had done. I needed something to calm me down a little. 'Wow,' I said.

Pernilla looked at the ring, whose three large diamonds sparkled in the pub's lights. 'You were clever to ask first and give me the ring later. I might have just said yes for the ring,' she said.

We had to tell someone. So we walked ten minutes to the home where my mother lived and paid a surprise visit.

'Mum, we're getting married.'

'Oh, that is good,' she said when we told her. She got up from her armchair and kissed Pernilla.

'You're the first person we've told, Mum,' I said.

'Yes,' she said, as if she expected nothing less.

'And, look, I gave her Granny McAllester's engagement ring,' I said, pointing to the antique sparkles on Pernilla's finger, the ring my father's mother had worn.

'That was meant to belong to me, you know,' my mother said.

'Mum,' I said, staring her down.

My mother, with some effort, veered back to civility.

'It looks beautiful on you, Pernilla. Now I would like some grandchildren, please.'

I had always dreaded my wedding because I knew my mother would almost certainly spoil it. She would have to be in the same building, the same room, as my father for hours on end. The chances of unpleasantness occurring were extremely high. My sister and I had talked about our future weddings for years. We had long ago agreed that one of us would be getting married while the other would be shadowing our mother like a police officer watching a prisoner who has been let out for an afternoon.

'You know, it's kind of great that she's not going to be there,' I told Pernilla one day as we sat at our dining table designing invitations.

'No, it's not,' Pernilla said. 'That's ridiculous.'

'OK, but it's great that she's not around to piss me off while we plan all this stuff. She doesn't get a vote on anything. And believe me, she would have tried.'

Pernilla didn't say anything.

'Honestly,' I said.

Pernilla and I were married ten months after my mother died, on 18 March 2006 at Chelsea Old Town Hall.

The morning of the wedding I remembered a conversation I had with my mother when I was about seven as we drove along a road near our flat in Edinburgh. We were talking about the day I was born.

'That was one of the happiest days of my life,' my mother said.

'Wasn't it the happiest?' I asked, mildly offended.

'No, the happiest day of my life was the day I married Daddy,' she said.

I remained somewhat put out by that. But on the day I married Pernilla I think I understood what my mother had felt about her own wedding day.

My sister and father and I and everyone else there who knew of my mother's volatility were able to relax. But for all her destructive capability, I would have done anything to have had her there. Bound and gagged, perhaps.

Coming home from school in Edinburgh

13

After my mother died, I hired a carpenter to build shelves in the home that Pernilla and I had bought the month of my mother's death. I wanted to fill an alcove in the kitchen with shelves for my cookery books. The carpenter puzzled over how to fit the design around an inconvenient radiator that poked into the alcove along the side wall. 'We could have a little column of smaller shelves above the raditor, pressed up against the wall,' he said, after staring for a while at the space. 'Perfect for a few paperbacks.'

That was where I put most of my mother's cookery books when I took them home from my sister's. Slightly separated by the carpentry from their new, glossy successors, the old paperbacks were held together by tape and stuck together in places by years-old splotches of sauce and fat and gravy. That corner of the kitchen, hidden behind the door, became my reference library, taking me back to the past.

I read my mother's cookery books without much direction from my memory. Not many of the recipes in Elizabeth David seemed familiar to me. My initial memories of my mother's food were of simpler dishes, aimed at children more than at adults. But these were the books my mother had commanded me to read, and so I decided to choose recipes from them as they appealed to me, as she must have chosen dishes. I chose cassoulet, if only because it seemed the quintessence of hearty French cooking, a dish to be shared with family and friends. It would be the first dish I would attempt to master.

Two days after I left Lebanon, I took down *French Country Cooking* from the kitchen shelf to which I had returned it upon coming home, and read how to make cassoulet. Elizabeth David, in her slightly irritating snobbishness, doesn't bother to translate the passage from Anatole France with which she opens her two-page recipe for 'Le Cassoulet de Castelnaudary', but I could more or less work out that it is about a small tavern, owned by a woman named Clémence, where there is only one dish on the menu. It's been that way for twenty years. From time to time, France writes, Clémence changes some of the ingredients in the cassoulet, 'mais c'est toujours le même cassoulet'. It is always the same cassoulet. What remains constant in Clémence's cassoulet, he writes, is the base.

How can it be the same if it changes? I had tried making changes to various recipes in the cookery books I had used over the years. It had not resulted in making anything you could describe as 'toujours le même'. Toujours ruined, perhaps. So I had learned never to deviate. Ever.

Elizabeth David might have been surprised to hear of the existence of those who follow cookery books 'in every detail', as she writes, but we are many. The novelist Julian Barnes – who is one himself – calls us 'pedants in the kitchen'. We follow recipes. And I had become OK at it. I could pretty much put the right ingredients together at the right time and at the right temperature. By the end of the process I would have read the recipe, always open on the table in the centre of the kitchen, perhaps a dozen times. An hour later, I would remember nothing. I had merely been following instructions. It was not very difficult. When I cooked I was reading a map in a foreign city I knew I'd never revisit. There were so many great recipes in all the books that lined my shelves. Thousands, perhaps tens of thousands of amazing recipes to try out. Why, I had always thought, would I waste my time cooking any of them again?

One Sunday in London, shortly after I moved there in late

2003, I cooked lunch for my friends, starting with 'Sautéed Shrimp with Orange Dust', a recipe I found in a book by New York's master of fusion, Jean-Georges Vongerichten. Orange dust sounded fantastic to me. I made it, and it stuck nicely to the shrimp and tasted dustily orangey.

The next day I had but the vaguest memory of what orange dust actually was. To make it again, I would have had to open the book and start from scratch. To make an omelette, for that matter, I'd have had to open the book.

My food generally worked out, but it was not the result of what my mother – and many other people who seemed to be able to enter a grocery shop without a list and a kitchen without a book splayed open on the worktop from start to finish – would call cooking. My form of cooking and shopping was inseparable from words on the page.

I just read out instructions and shopping lists to myself and the dishes appeared after a lot of rereading. It was like using foreign words looked up in a dictionary. I could pronounce the words and I could understand them, but I couldn't remember them and I certainly couldn't string them together in anything that resembled speaking.

Julian Barnes seems to be happily resigned to this condition. But every time I remembered my mother's mild taunt about keeping the recipe book closed, I felt more and more like a fraudulent cook. And to make matters worse, I knew that my pedantry could turn to tyranny. Cooking by rote is, after all, primarily about controlling every detail.

Only months after meeting me, even before we got married, Pernilla began to dread my urges to cook for people. 'When gourmandism is shared, it has the most marked influence on the happiness which can be found in marriage,' writes Jean-Anthelme Brillat-Savarin in *The Physiology of Taste*.

Yes – when it is shared.

I would choose recipes with ingredients like orange dust in them and invite too many people for my capabilities. I would become very stressed as the time of the guests' arrival approached if matters were not entirely in line with how the recipe said they should be. My spousal manners were not always what they might have been.

'I don't like you when you're cooking,' Pernilla said one day. 'I don't think we should have any more dinner parties.'

'But I'm cooking because I want to make people happy,' I said.

'You're not making me happy,' she said. 'You're a dictator.'

She was right. Nor was cooking for many people under the sort of pressure Jack Bauer works under in an episode of 24 making me particularly happy. The occasional oohs and aahs that came in the wake of orange-dusted shrimp satisfied my ego, I suppose, but it was not exactly fun and celebratory.

Once, without any sense of irony, I told my friend John that he wasn't 'cutting the onions properly'. And when my wife was cooking, some impulse pushed me into the kitchen to stand at her side and say things like: 'You need to stir the pasta more often. It's sticking together.' Or: 'I think the heat is up a bit high.'

'Get – away – from – me,' she would say. Sometimes she would use less decorous phrases to precipitate my departure.

My mother, in her genuine concern that her only son needed to end up married to someone who cooked for him, had an unfortunate habit of repeatedly asking Pernilla what she liked to cook whenever we went round to see her. I would watch Pernilla tense up, ever so slightly, when asked this question. And in my mind's eye I could see her inch ever further away from the stove. 'I often do a whole salmon, or risotto,' Pernilla would say, begrudgingly.

Screw this, she was clearly saying to herself.

'Mum, I barely let her in the kitchen,' I said during one visit, which was both the truth and a way of saving Pernilla from having to produce an answer so fine-tuned as to be both right-eously feminist and balm to her future mother-in-law.

My mother wouldn't let it drop. She never let things drop. Her eyebrows were still raised as she looked at Pernilla.

'But you must cook when Matthew's away,' she said. 'And what about when you have babies?'

'Yes, it'll be difficult when he's away so much,' Pernilla said. 'I'm not going to stop working so we'll have to get a nanny, for sure.'

This seemed to be the right answer. My mother settled down a bit.

'Oh yes, Pernilla, servants can make excellent company, you know,' she said, cigarette smoke billowing out of her mouth with each uttered syllable.

'We don't really call them servants these days, Mum,' I said, laughing.

The cooking interrogation was over – for now.

It is possible, I suppose, that I inherited my control issues in the kitchen from my mother, one of the bossiest people to have walked the earth. Wherever they came from, I sensed that I needed to work on losing my Saddam tendencies now that I was trying to follow her from-the-grave insistence that I learn to cook with the book closed. Perhaps she was suggesting posthumously how I might not only learn to cook but learn to enjoy cooking. I used to think about Saddam a lot – it was part of my job – and at one point I decided that even before he was toppled during the invasion of Iraq he was probably the most trapped and fearful person in the country. He was scared of nearly everyone. Being a dictator was not actually much fun after a while. Chefs say that you must cook with love, that the diners can taste it in the food. I cooked with the stress and restless fear of the tyrant, and I'm sure you could taste that too. My mother – and quite a few others around the world – cooked with love. I had to learn that trick.

There was something about going back to French food, to the Mediterranean cooking that Elizabeth David and then my mother had learned and revelled in, that made me feel as though I was beginning again at the beginning – of food, of feeding. I could not help feeling that there was no cuisine as fundamentally joyful and somehow attached to the earth, to other people, as Mediterranean, particularly French food. Mediterranean food is about meals, not dishes; ritual celebrations, not one-time events; home cooking, not restaurant cooking; long, unfolding afternoons in the outdoors, not hurried dinners in city dining rooms; flowers and herbs growing around the table on the patio, not flowers arranged at the end of the dining room. It is about families and friends and welcoming newcomers. It's about giving, not showing off; feeding people rather than dazzling them. It suggests memories we're not even sure we really have. Perhaps they're ancestral memories or memories we long to build up.

Until now I had flitted around the globe in my kitchen as much as in my working life. My cooking was like my languages. I could say 'thank you', 'hello' and 'journalist' in many languages, but I couldn't speak any fluently. On my kitchen bookshelves was a UN-like multinational force of cookery books – Thai, Indian, Moroccan, Spanish, French, American, English, Scottish, Italian, Persian and Indonesian. And dessert. I realized that I could cook nothing with any authority. So I closed my ears to the babble of exotic tongues on my shelves and listened only to the Latins. It was a relief to narrow down the world of food a little bit. Elizabeth David wrote mainly for housewives in the post-war era. As I read her recipes, I found that she makes assumptions that would sit easily with women who spend all day cooking for their families – or for people, like me, who have made a deliberate decision to slow down, stay rooted and cook. She assumes, for example, that you always have home-made chicken and beef stock at hand. That assumption implies days of preparation, including roasting whole joints of meat for other meals before the one you are now making. There is no short cut to that, other than the shame of the stock cube or the tinned variety.

To make proper stock – and it really is incomparable with the thin dribble produced by stock cubes and superior to anything from a tin – you have to buy big pieces of meat, roast them, eat them, save the bones, buy lots of celery you will never need once you've put a few sticks into the stockpot, boil the stuff for hours (so no going out to buy a pint of milk and no going out to earn a living) and freeze it in Tupperware.

Want to make a cassoulet? Don't even think about it before you've spent two or three days shopping, cooking, eating and boiling as described above. Because cassoulet, I discovered, needs stock.

The more I read Elizabeth David's recipes and the beautiful snippets of culinary history she weaves between her recipes, the more I realized that it was going to take time to learn to cook like my mother. I needed to be cooking a lot, and slowly. Roasts beget bones, which beget stock, which begets soup. Meals that were once, for me, unconnected now began to be reliant upon one another.

I read further in the long recipe for cassoulet de Castelnaudary to discover that 'Toulouse, Carcassonne, Périgord, Castelnaudary, Gascony, Castannau, all have their own version of the Cassoulet. The ingredients vary from fresh pork and mutton to smoked sausages, garlic sausages, bacon, smoked ham, preserved goose or pork, duck, calves' feet, the rind of pork and pigs' cheek.' But which? How do you choose? How do you get it right? I do not happen to be from, nor have I ever visited, any of these places in the south-west of France. Where should my loyalties lie?

'The essentials are good white haricot beans and a capacious earthenware pot (the name Cassoulet comes from Cassol d'Issel, the original clay cooking utensil from the little town of Issel, near Castelnaudary).'

My initial confusion began to fade with those words. I started to feel that this one recipe – in fact, even just the Anatole France passage – hinted at more to me than almost anything I'd ever read about cooking. I hadn't really understood that cooking had a base, but now I could see it. And so the impossible feat of memory I had assumed was required for cooking such as my mother did – how on earth did one memorize a thousand measurements, ingredients, cooking times, temperatures? – began to retreat a little.

'Remember the base,' I thought to myself. 'Good beans and an earthenware pot.'

That didn't stop me from making a detailed, panicky list as I headed out shopping. My progress, I sensed, would be slow. Like much of French cooking itself.

Top of the list was a cassoulet pot.

'Can I help you?' the lady in the kitchen shop in Swiss Cottage asked me.

'I'm looking for a cassoulet dish,' I said.

I was not entirely sure what they looked like, but I thought I had spotted a few likely earthenware candidates. This lady would know.

She took me to the window and pointed at a big copper dish that looked like a clam. And cost a fortune.

'No,' I said. 'For making cassoulet. They're clay, aren't they?'

'Well, that,' she said, looking at the copper clam, 'is a cassoulet.'

This was all going wrong already. I thought cassoulet was something you ate. This lady was saying that it was the pot itself. And the wrong kind of pot. 'But Elizabeth David says I need a capacious earthenware pot,' I wanted to tell this nice woman, who I'm sure knew what she was talking about. But so did Elizabeth David. And Elizabeth David did not say I should buy a metal dish that looked like a clam and cost one hundred pounds.

'Do you have any earthenware ones?' I asked, veering toward the dishes I'd been looking at earlier. They were a fraction of the cost of the clam – and would require no polishing.

'You could use this one,' she said. I felt happier. She had taken me back to the earthenware-pot section. I took the most capacious one they had. And the lady sold me a circular flat metal thing that, she said, would prevent my nice new pot from cracking when I placed it on direct heat.

I drove to Clifton Road in Little Venice. This neighbourhood in north-west London is now the turf of many of London's super-rich. But in the late 1960s and early 1970s it wasn't quite as swanky. We lived there. My first and second homes, on Elizabeth Close and Ashworth Road, are both a short walk to the shops on Clifton Road. I have a handful of memories of living in the neighbourhood – standing in the street on Ashworth Road and looking up at the purple curtains in my bedroom window, looking down at the canal boats, dropping my sister off at play school, meeting a basset hound in a park – and there are photos of me in the garden there. But I knew now that my mother used to come to these shops to buy food for me, the first food I ever ate. Sometimes in her last years, my sister told me later, my mother would return to sit and drink coffee alone in a café on Clifton Road, looking out at the streets where she had been sane and at her happiest. It seemed right to buy the food for this meal here.

In the delicatessen I found cassoulet essential number two – a big jar of white haricot beans. They were already soaked and prepared. With pork stock in the freezer (serendipitously made after a recent pork roast) and the capacious earthenware pot in my car, I felt that I was halfway there. I looked around and there was a tin of confit de canard. It was not the preserved goose that Elizabeth David's cassoulet of Castelnaudary demands, but I felt sure it was on her list of regional change-ables. 'Duck will do,' I thought. As I was paying for it, I realized I had just bought off the list. I had extemporized. It was probably a bad idea. But I couldn't be bothered looking for goose when duck was at hand.

The sausages came from the newly opened organic butcher

across the street. I'd never been in the shop before. I thought about how often my mother must have come here when this shop was Cobb of Knightsbridge, one of London's finest butchers, supplier of meat to the Queen. I assumed Elizabeth David shopped here too. And that thought prompted a memory of something I'd read somewhere in her books.

'Can I have some bones, please?' I asked the butcher.

'What kind?'

'I don't know. Whatever you have.'

He looked at me.

'Pork?' I suggested.

He cut some up with a cleaver and put them in a plastic bag and charged me nothing. And even though I'd read it in books before – to get bones for stock, just ask your butcher – those passively read words had never quite turned into action when faced with a shop full of dead animals. Now, in this one moment, I'd skipped entire phases of making stock – the buying, roasting and eating of a piece of meat. I could keep the frozen stock for another time.

In the kitchen at home, I made fresh stock with the bones the butcher had given me. When it was ready, I began to slice onions and bacon and tomatoes; I crushed garlic; I put them together in a pan with herbs and salt and pepper. The salt I got from my mother's huge blue-and-white salt jar by reaching in with my whole hand. When I was a kid I used to think it would bite my hand off. The herbs were from my garden. Again a loose end struck me – Elizabeth David's list of ingredients does not actually include herbs. But I'd gone downstairs to the garden and snipped some thyme from its terracotta pot and rosemary from the gnarly bush in the flower bed, my fingers happily scented with the cosy, familiar smells of the Mediterranean. I was making my own decision on the ingredients. For the second time in one dish. I poured the stock over it all and let it simmer, as Elizabeth David instructs, for twenty minutes.

From this point it was bizarrely easy. I rubbed the pot with a sliced clove of garlic, the raw, almost-white root giving its delicious moistness to the surface of the earthenware as my pursed fingertips pushed and slid it around the glazed clay. And then I dumped the sausages, bits of bacon, duck confit – it just slid out of its jar with all its congealed fat – and some goose fat into the garlicky-smelling earthenware pot. On top of that I poured the beans. And then the stock, with all its good herby vegetable bits.

And then I defied Elizabeth David. And France. I skipped the breadcrumb-layer-on-top bit. I don't really like breadcrumbs.

Pernilla and Richard Poureshagh, a dear friend going back to my days at primary school in Edinburgh, sat around our dining table and could not stop saying how 'light' the cassoulet was.

I said nothing. I knew what had gone into this earthenware dish.

'I'm just not in the mood for something heavy – it's summer,' Rich said. We had just come back from a bacchanalian Sunday afternoon at the Notting Hill Carnival, an event as far from the carnage of Lebanon as it was possible to get. Or from the oil war being waged by guerrillas in the Niger Delta region in Nigeria, where I was due to go in a few days.

'Totally light,' Pernilla said, and they accepted spoonfuls more of the stuff.

'That's how hot, melted fat goes,' I said to myself. It seems light as it slips down. It is shockingly heavy when it congeals. It is joyous.

So cassoulet was the first dish I cooked with a bit of the flexibility and the joy that I wanted to bring into my kitchen. A bit more like the way my mother cooked.

The first dish of a hundred, I decided in the next moment. I would create my own recipe book for my own repertoire. A book that, once completed, I would never need to look at again. In theory. Once I had filled it with a hundred recipes that I could make without actually opening the notebook itself, I would have fulfilled my mother's challenge.

I bought a beautiful, leather-bound brown notebook. Trying my best to remember the details of cassoulet without consulting Elizabeth David – not entirely successfully – I began to fill out the first page of my recipe book.

'Take an egg in your hand,' I remembered my mother saying. Jane and I were standing in the kitchen in Edinburgh and open on the worktop was our first ever cookery book: *Look! I Can Cook* by Angela Burdick. The cover featured a naughty-looking little boy with freckles and red hair, a slightly older girl and a sensible, flared-trousers-wearing older boy. The red-haired boy's tongue was licking his upper, smiling lip and his tummy was exposed over his yellow shorts. He was rubbing his hands together in anticipation. That was the character I liked.

'Crack it against the rim of the bowl and then tip the egg into the bowl,' my mother said, and she broke an egg with one hand and tipped its slinky contents into the bowl.

'I don't like eggs, Mum,' I said. 'I hate them.'

'But you and Jane are making a Spanish Omelette,' she said. 'Omelettes aren't like normal eggs. They're not eggy at all, actually.'

'I like omelettes,' Jane said, which annoyed me.

So I broke my first eggs. For all the fried onion, tomato and green pepper folded inside it, the omelette tasted pretty eggy to me. Cooking, I decided, was for girls.

❧

Cassoulet

There are three parts to this, none of them difficult.

First, the beans. If you don't simply buy them in a jar, you soak one and a half to two pounds of dried white haricot beans in a big bowl of water overnight. The next day you rinse them, put them in a pan of fresh water, and cook them for two and a half hours or so – until they're three-quarters cooked. Strain them.

A slightly more involved recipe given by Elizabeth David – 'Cassoulet Toulousain' – requires you to cook the beans with onion, garlic, pork rind, a piece of thick-cut bacon and a bunch of herbs, including parsley, thyme and a bay leaf.

Of course, going to your deli and buying a lovely, ready-made jar of white haricot beans so you don't need to bother soaking or cooking at all is a very good cheat. I recommend it.

Second, make a stock.

Slice three onions, cut half a pound of bacon into smallish squares, slice five cloves of garlic, two tomatoes, add seasoning and some herbs of your choice (I'd go for thyme or rosemary), add the stock, and let all that cook for twenty minutes in a pan.

Finally, take the earthenware cassoulet pot or dish and rub the inside of it with a clove of garlic. Just slice a clove in half and use the exposed end. Then dump the following into the pot, in no particular order: the bacon bits from the stock (if you can be bothered taking them all out), a pound of good sausages and as much goose or duck fat from the confit or separate jars or tins of the stuff as you think necessary. Pour the beans over that delicious mish-mash. And the stock goes over it all.

Cook in a medium to hot oven for an hour.

You can sprinkle breadcrumbs over it at the end, but I'm not sure I see the point.

I'd eat it with a simple green salad and a big red wine, perhaps a bottle from Cahors in the south-west of France – or a bottle of Malbec from Mendoza in Argentina. (It's the same grape in both places. Either is usually heavenly.)

14

The therapist was right about the first anniversary. I hadn't thought that such an arbitrary mark of time could have much power. I wished that my grief didn't conform to a pattern. It felt unique to me, not something I shared with others who had gone through something similar. It was brutal, physical in its strength.

Jane emailed during the day to say she had cried at work.

My aunt Kata called and she sounded lonely without her sister to talk to. Even though she said she still spoke to my mother sometimes in person, in her living room, it was not quite the same as being able to pick up the phone for a chat.

Pernilla, desperately worried about her father, who lay sick with cancer in Vancouver, was gentle and patient. She listened and knew that that was all that I needed.

I had no grave to visit so in the afternoon I went to the Waitrose on Finchley Road and on the way there I took a detour and drove on to Eton Avenue, where Rathmore House sits. I had avoided driving along the road since my mother had died. I glanced up at her window. There were the pink horse chestnut flowers, in their brief blossom. I didn't stop the car. I felt like a stalker of the dead.

15

As I began to cook my mother's food, I realized her recipes would take me only so far. During some of her happiest years I was either an infant or not yet born. I had to reach beyond my memories as well as into them. And so I turned my skills and effort as a reporter away from war and towards my mother. I began to spend hours talking to my father, to my mother's three siblings, to my sister. And as they spoke with an ease I had never seen when my mother was alive, I realized that my mother had to die before I could get to know who she was. When she was alive, those happy years remained largely hidden, an unbearably sad reminder – to herself, to those who loved her – of all she had lost.

'You see, I was living in the States by that time so I didn't see it early on – the first I heard was when I spoke to Mummy on the phone and she told me that they'd been having problems with Ann,' Jennifer told me as we sat around one Sunday afternoon in Newport in early 2007, my tape recorder running on the coffee table. 'Mummy said that Ann had refused to take you and Jane round any more, that she was just very hostile.'

'When did you first see her nuttiness yourself?' I asked.

'Oh, I remember when she threw me out of the car. I was in Edinburgh and we were coming back from a birthday party or something. You must have been about eight or nine.'

'It was the trampoline centre in Portobello,' I said, suddenly remembering.

'That's right. And we were on a road next to Arthur's Seat in the car and your mother started to get very angry with me. And Jane was in the back seat saying, "Mummy, please." And then she threw me out! I had to get a bus back to Mummy and Daddy's.'

We spoke for hours, laughing at my mother's oddness until the conversation turned to my teenage years and then we agreed to end the conversation there. 'Do you really want to talk about all that?' Jennifer asked me.

'No, let's not,' I said, and we both breathed a sigh of relief.

My father, I'm sure, would never have been as open if she had still been alive. Now, I sensed it was a release for him to be able to talk about the woman with whom he had chosen to have children and to build a life, until she had gone crazy. 'No one else will ever ask him about this,' I thought.

Even when I asked him about the toughest of times, he never hesitated to respond. 'I do remember that after the second [ECT, or electric shock] treatment she asked me not to let them do it again,' he recalled in an email in October 2007, when I had probed him for details about my mother's medical treatment. 'She just didn't want them messing with her head again and she was genuinely quite frightened.' My questions sparked good memories too, about their first years together, and her first attempts in the kitchen. There was no haute cuisine in those days: 'Spaghetti bolognaise and that sort of thing,' my father said.

One evening when they were first in London they had a friend called Gerda over for dinner. My mother made chilli con carne. They all took a couple of forkfuls of the stuff before agreeing that it was inedibly hot. They had bread and cheese instead. It was around this time that my mother bought her first Katie Stewart book, soon followed by her first Elizabeth David. She needed, clearly, some help.

My mother's cooking improved steadily throughout the sixties, the era of the dinner party. She had no career to speak of and I imagine she felt the need of an arena in which she could excel.

'There was definitely a strong competitive thing going on with the women and honour was very much at stake,' my father recalled. 'Mum soon got the reputation of being one of the better cooks. The preparation for such events was seriously serious. One learned to keep out of the way as her short fuse was inclined to get a bit shorter.'

Away from the kitchen, my parents explored the increasingly good restaurants of London in the sixties, eating out about once a week: 369 on the Kings Road, Geales in Notting Hill for its legendary fish and chips, La Poissonerie de l'Avenue in Chelsea, Robert Carrier's restaurant and once, when someone else was paying, Le Gavroche.

'Mum was given a menu with no prices on and everything she chose was the most expensive,' my father remembered. 'When it came to the sweets she chose something with wild strawberries from somewhere exotic. I was trying to nudge her under the table to deflect her but failed.'

As well as my conversations with my family, there were documents. Along with her cookery books were family home movies I had never seen and a large collection of beautiful family photographs taken by my father, a black-and-white chronicle of captured moments that ends suddenly when I am about ten years old.

I sat and watched the cine films, which my father had had transferred to DVD: and there he was, thinner and much younger, hiding behind trees near Kenwood House on Hampstead Heath; and my mother, pushing a huge pram along the pavement in Little Venice; and my scrunched-up infant face; and a panning shot of Port an Droighionn, recorded when my father and Dominic discovered the bay. I flicked through page after page of photographs of us all, most of them of Jane and me: hand in hand on a country lane; running naked around the garden in Ashworth Road; sitting on a potty looking out to the sea at Port an Droighionn before the house was built.

I remembered that I, too, had a small archive. In my father's garage was a box full of every letter I ever received up until the age of about twenty. I had another box somewhere, I suspected, of the letters that came later. Many would be from my mother. And on my computer I had many of my own letters.

'I think she [Jane] and I are both ready to deal with Mum dying. I think. In many ways, if not all,' I wrote to my father in 1999, from Jerusalem, as news of my mother's enlarged liver – from drinking – reached me from Jane. Much more alcohol, her doctors had told her, and she could develop cirrhosis, which would probably kill her. 'I think a lot about the sadness of her having her life and personality snatched away by madness … My memories of her, I'm afraid, are now just ones of madness.'

I also had my diaries, which I began to keep when I was about ten and continued for a decade. They would be turgid and solipsistic, the product of my teens, but perhaps they would spark memories of my mother.

And one day my sister mentioned my mother's papers. I had no idea there were any. I drove over and picked up two portable box files and one small suitcase. But, like my mother's own recipe book, I left them undisturbed. Much as I wanted to see what they had to tell me, I wasn't ready.

See-sawing in the garden at Ashworth Road

16

One night in the summer of 2006, during a visit to Israel to cover the conflict I knew more intimately than any other, I was sitting at a bar in Jerusalem with my friend Matt. A pregnant woman was sitting next to me. I was eating a steak salad.

'Is that good?' she asked me.

'Yeah, do you want some? I've had enough.'

'Sure,' she said, and I slid it over to her.

She ate it all.

'There,' said Matt, to whom I had just explained both my urge to learn to cook using my mother's cookery books until I could do it according to her definition of proper cooking and the difficulty my wife and I faced in having a child. Pernilla and I had given it our best shot, making a baby, but it wasn't happening the natural way. My not being around for half the year – and often at precisely the wrong time for conception – did not improve our already biologically lowered chances. 'You've just fed a child. That's what it's all about, really, isn't it? You want to feed your own child.'

He was right. And so my cooking took on another purpose. Once back in London, where I had already been cooking to find my way back to the past, I now began to see cooking as a path to a hoped-for future. I began to read about the impact of diet on unborn and newborn children and about researchers in Pennsylvania who had discovered that even our future taste preferences are partially formed in the womb. After three months, the taste buds of a foetus are almost fully developed. If strong flavours like cumin, garlic and onion meander through the amniotic fluid to the unborn child, out comes a little boy or girl who will tend to like cumin, garlic, onion or whatever strong-flavoured foods they've been fed before they've even seen the light of day. All of it, of course, going through the mother. I couldn't do much more than take vitamins and cut back on the booze to boost the number and swimming skills of my sperm. Pernilla had a whole lot more to deal with. We were moving on to in vitro fertilization, a process that can be very unpleasant for a woman. So the least I could do was to keep her very well fed. I reckoned some well-directed French food could help build her body into a receptive place for a child, and, once the child was inside there, I could start feeding it. I wanted it to grow up big and strong and with a distinct liking for estouffade de boeuf à la Provençale.

Or steak with bordelaise sauce. In preparation for our first IVF attempt, the doctors and nurses at the fertility clinic insisted that both Pernilla and I consume as much protein as possible. Immediately after hearing the recommendation, my mind started to wander to The Ginger Pig, an extraordinary butcher in Marylebone that sells the best beef I've ever tasted in Britain. It's dry-aged for at least twenty-eight days, and the butchers will position their hacksaws on the joints wherever you want them to. 'A little wider, please.' The steaks are enormous, leaping with beefiness to the extent that mustard or garlic butter would be an insult to the meat, and the raw flesh sinks under the pressure of your thumb and only slowly resumes its shape. So that's what I cooked for us and for friends on the first Saturday of May 2007.

The evening before, Pernilla and I had walked through Queen's Park into a shaded area the park managers keep in an inner-city version of countryside wildness.

'So what are the bags and the rubber gloves for?' Pernilla asked.

'Nettles,' I said. 'We're going to have nettle soup.'

'Eww, what about all the dog pee on them? And won't they be covered in pollution?' Pernilla said.

'Nah, they'll be fine. Just keep an eye out for the parkies.'

Waist-high nettles lined the path. I snapped on a yellow rubber glove, pulled out a pair of scissors I had brought, and began filling the plastic bags with the nettles.

Pernilla looked around to make sure we weren't being watched. 'Let me try,' she said.

I had shopped for everything else – the huge T-bones, some marrow bones from The Ginger Pig to make Elizabeth David's bordelaise sauce for the incredible steaks, cream and coffee beans for her mocha glacé (an odd, simple way of making the purest coffee ice cream) and two bottles of rosé prosecco. And I had called the wonderful Golborne Fisheries fishmonger and asked them to keep a lobster for me the next morning.

One day we should feast on lobster and tankards of pink champagne as Bond does in *From Russia with Love*, my friend John had emailed me that week, apropos of nothing, and I silently decided that that's what we would start with.

I had never cooked a lobster. But for once I knew exactly how to do it, without even looking in a book, let alone keeping it open.

As I drove home with the thing thrashing about in a bag on the passenger seat next to me, I could see my mother standing in the kitchen in Ardnamurchan, picking up the nice blue lobster we had pulled out of the sea in a creel, dropping it into a big pan of boiling water, hearing a high-pitched whine, and looking in to see an entirely pink lobster. And an entirely dead one. 'I hate this part,' she would say.

'Just stick it in a pan of boiling water,' the fishmonger confirmed.

What he neglected to say was how I should keep the thing alive in the meantime. So I got all innovative and humane – before the merciless slaughter – and filled a big bowl full of cold water and sea salt and put it in the fridge. From another room we could hear its well-armoured tail and legs clinking against the glass of the bowl.

'That poor lobster,' Pernilla said.

'It's obviously happy,' I thought.

Ten minutes later the clinking stopped. I opened the fridge door a bit later. The lobster was motionless and did not stir when I picked it up. I had managed to drown it. Shit. Could you even eat pre-killed lobster? I called the fishmonger.

'Yeah, that will have killed it,' he said when I explained what I had done.

'But I was trying to give it a happy last few hours,' I wanted to say. A bit of the Atlantic in my fridge.

'Oh,' I said. 'Will it be OK to eat?'

'Absolutely,' he said.

Our friends came, among them Sophie, my ex-girlfriend. She was very pregnant – with an IVF baby whose maker was the same doctor at work on our efforts. I was cooking for the unborn, for her baby, and hopefully for ours, preparing a protein-filled home to welcome it.

'You know, if this works, the baby will be an Aquarius,' Pernilla said, as I fired up the barbecue.

'As long as it's human,' I said.

It was amazing steak that my wife put into her body that afternoon.

❧

Entrecôte à la Bordelaise

The only thing that really, really matters when cooking steak is buying it. I'm not the first person to say that, but still, spend big. If it's not that great, steak becomes a bit of a task about a quarter of the way through the eating. With great steak, you never want it to end and you never really feel full.

It's hard to beat a very good steak with absolutely nothing on it at all. No mustard, no sauce, no garlic butter. But a bordelaise sauce, which is really just another form of cow meat, is an exception because it actually enhances the steak-ness of the steak. It doesn't compete with the meat or distract you from the meat. It is a loyal friend to the meat.

Bordelaise is just chopped shallots, beef marrow and chopped parsley. Elizabeth David, in *French Provincial Cooking*, recommends buying the marrow bones a day before the meal so you can soak them in cold water, changing the water several times. This keeps the marrow nice and pink, whereas normally it's a rather unappetizing grey. When you're ready, boil the three-inch-long pieces of marrow bone for twenty minutes and then scoop out the marrow.

Spread the marrow, shallot and parsley mixture on top of the steak as it is being grilled.

17

The next morning I parked on a quiet street in central London, the city all but empty at this early hour on a Sunday, and Pernilla burst into song.

'This is the dawning of the age of Aquarius,' she sang, through her laughter. 'Aquaaaarius.'

It was, of all dates, 6 May 2007, the second anniversary of my mother's death. I found it hard not to wonder if this wasn't auspicious, if there wasn't a rightness in the well-ordered demise of one person and the creation of another exactly two years later. I had initially bridled at the one-size-fits-all two-year milestone of feeling better that the shrink had described, but perhaps, like it or not, anniversaries do have resonance. Perhaps my grief wasn't actually so unusual. Perhaps it was something universal. I had definitely filed down its sharper edges with my cooking, and my time in the kitchen had repeatedly allowed me to reach back to a time when my mother had been a force for unsullied good in my life, and I was beginning to feel less tied down by grief. As, perhaps, anyone would after two years. And now there was this coincidence of death and creation, the sense that the vacuum left in the world when my mother left it could be filled by the little things Pernilla and I were about to create, and that shaded an anniversary of loss with excitement.

Pernilla and I entered the white town house in Marylebone, the clinic of the richest doctor in Britain. He and his fellow doctors were Egyptians, and that made me feel oddly at home, a team from my old Middle Eastern haunts working on something so domestic and personal. Pernilla was taken downstairs to the basement while I sat in the waiting room among all the would-be pregnant and newly pregnant mothers staring into the home-decoration and gossip magazines that lay in rows on the coffee table in the centre of the room. I waited for the would-be father upstairs to finish his part of the equation. After a long while I became anxious, assuming that he had finished and left his sample behind and that the team of pretty, blonde Australian nurses in the office had forgotten to come into the waiting room to tell me it was my turn in the jerk-off bathroom. Given the harvesting of my wife's eggs that was going on right now in the basement of the clinic, I reckoned it was important that my part in this procedure was done on time. So I picked up my bag, which contained a transparent cup and a brown paper bag, and I cornered one of the nurses.

'Um, I've been waiting rather a long time. I'm just worried you've forgotten about me.'

'No, no, the other guy's just finished.'

I gave her a look of surprise – had he been struck by stage fright, or was he just concocting incredibly elaborate doctors-and-nurses fantasies up there? – and she smiled.

'We'll call you through in a minute.'

Afterwards, I read the paper in a café on Marylebone High Street and had breakfast while I waited for Pernilla. Across the street was Divertimenti, one of Elizabeth David's favourite kitchen shops. As the embryologist at the clinic was extracting Pernilla's eggs and pairing them with my sperm, doing the job of conception on our behalf, I began to think about what I should cook for Sunday dinner. I needed to provide comfort and health for Pernilla, something homely and full of the protein her doctors insisted on her consuming as if she were bulking up for the Ms Olympia contest. My mother would roast a chicken, I knew. The ultimate crowd-pleaser. The farmers' market in Queen's Park is on Sunday mornings, and a farmer there sells wonderful chickens that have run around fields and eaten good things all their lives. As we drove to the farmers' market from the clinic, I asked Pernilla if she wouldn't mind if we made a small detour to Eton Avenue.

This time I drove slowly. I did not feel the need to rush past the place where my mother had died. Today was a good day. There could be little room for sadness.

Eton Avenue is a quiet, broad street and it was an unhurried morning there, so I idled the car and looked up. And there were the pink flowers again, marking the loveliest moment of spring, when the most graceful of trees fill the parks and fields of England with clusters of white and pink flowers that sway among the rustle of the thick, freshly green chestnut leaves splaying out in clusters below. There's no moment of the year that is more full of life. The brief appearance of the pink flowers would for ever mark the time of my mother's death, I realized. And now, perhaps, they would mark the time of her first grandchild's conception.

Pernilla's father had only recently died of cancer. Her pole-axing grief had come as strongly as my own.

'Help us, Ann and Dad,' Pernilla said as we drove away, and I silently echoed her, asking my mother and father-in-law for an assist. Not that I really believed they could help. They were dead. But you never know.

We stopped at the farmers' market and I bought a good, plump chicken.

Roasting chicken was the one thing I could do with my eyes – let alone the book – closed. I could insert slivers of garlic into the breast; I could coat it in harissa; I could cover it with a blizzard of Maldon Salt, pepper and herbs; I could – and this was my favourite – stuff the area between the breast and the skin with a prosciutto, butter, fresh herb, onion and Tuscan bread stuffing. All without opening a book (because once you've done any of these mind-bogglingly simple things, you basically just stick the bird in the oven and, an hour and a bit later, you take it out).

But perhaps my mother had found another way of roasting chicken in *French Provincial Cooking*, the book she called 'the Bible'. I flicked through and my eye stopped at 'Poulet Farci en Cocotte' – pot-roasted chicken with olive stuffing. I'd never pot-roasted anything before, and I was intrigued and attracted by Elizabeth David's promise: 'At the end of the cooking time the skin of the chicken is beautifully golden and crisp, and for once the legs will be cooked through as well as the breast.' Uncooked legs had not, as far as I was aware, ever been a problem with my oven-roasted chickens, but Elizabeth David's insistence made me want to try this. The last paragraph of this rather long recipe is a transparent provocation designed to lure you in, and it worked on me.

'I should add, perhaps, that the olive stuffing, although so good, is definitely rather odd', she writes. 'If the chicken is for guests with conventional tastes then it might be better to substitute a routine pork or herb stuffing.' And you may as well put down this book right now, you worthless, uncultured, parochial pond scum, she might have added.

Luckily, I had the cast-iron Le Creuset cocotte – just a large orange pan, really – that she suggests is ideal for pot-roasting.

I chopped some black olives, zinged some breadcrumbs in the food processor, diced an onion and chopped up a couple of sprigs of parsley I'd grown in a terracotta pot in the garden. With a beaten egg and some pepper, I squashed it all together in a bowl and stuffed it into the cavity of the chicken. This felt a bit old-fashioned and missed the point of having fatty, buttery stuffing seeping into the cooking flesh as it does when it's put between the skin and the meat, but it was also somehow reassuring to be stuffing a bird in the traditional way.

After that, I heated some olive oil in the pot, browned the chicken on both sides of the breast, covered it, and let it sit there on a low heat and in its own juices for an hour and twenty minutes or so.

When it was done, we ate it with reheated butternut squash

102

(mashed up with some maple syrup) I had barbecued the night before and some plain broccoli. Elizabeth David was right about the legs – they were more tender, more delicious than legs from an oven-roasted chicken. And the skin was brown, crispy and delicious. The stuffing was not, of course, in the slightest bit odd. I could remember how to do this with the book closed. I wrote the recipe in my repertoire notebook. The recipes in the book were growing in number.

One of the nurses called the next day to say that only three of the eight eggs had fertilized. We had hoped for a higher number of embryos.

'But, you know, there are now three little things in the world that we made,' I told Pernilla. 'It only takes one.'

On day three, they were ready. I felt as though this was all a glorious recipe and my wife's womb was the preheated oven. I kept this analogy to myself. One of the embryos had multiplied into seven cells, one into a whopping eight, and the runt of the litter five – it got left behind in the Petri dish. If it did well over the next few days, the clinic would freeze it.

We drove to the clinic. I held Pernilla's hand in the operating room. One doctor turned the lights down in the basement room, and the other squirted the two bigger embryos into my wife's uterus.

Nothing much actually happened. But it had the glorious shock of the new. And I was overcome with an urge to feed my wife, to feed the two embryos inside her, to keep them alive, to do my bit to make them grow, to give them strength. I couldn't do much – making a baby is woman's work, really – but I could shovel good nutrition towards them. Perhaps they could learn early to like a goat's cheese omelette made with free-range eggs, and velvety butternut-squash soup drizzled with white truffle oil and served with a slice of wholemeal organic toast with slivers of Parmesan on top and drizzled with a bit more of the truffle oil that I had picked up in Croatia during a recent trip. Because they were getting the omelette for their first lunch and the soup for their first dinner.

Before dinner, I ran around Queen's Park, and the world felt full of connections. For the Godless, connectivity is about the only meaning we can hope for. Connections can feel like the legs of a stool, keeping you up, keeping you stable. I played Kate Bush on my iPod. 'I know that something good is going to happen,' she sang, as I ran under the swaying horse-chestnut trees in the rain and wind. Spring itself felt like a connection, the right time to be planting and growing. I ran back through the rain to the kitchen. I never enjoyed making a meal more in my life.

✑

Goat's Cheese Omelette and Butternut Squash Soup with Truffle Oil and Parmesan Toast

For two people, use two full eggs and three yolks. Or two and two if you want. I prefer a yolky omelette. With a fork, gently beat the eggs in a bowl. Really, you're just mixing them up a bit. Drop little chunks of a soft goat's cheese into the mixture.

Heat some butter in a non-stick pan until it's sizzling, and then pour in the egg mixture.

You can use a spatula to lift one side of the omelette while you tip the pan so that the uncooked egg mixture slides under the bit you're lifting up. But don't flip the omelette like a pancake. The only turning over should be when you turn one half of the omelette over on the other – just before you take it out of the pan.

The soup I have stolen directly from Jamie Oliver. I saw him do it on television and never even needed to consult his book for the recipe – it's that simple.

Fry some sage leaves in olive oil. Take them out and put them aside.

Chop up a carrot, an onion, some garlic, some celery, a red chilli and rosemary, and cook in a pan for ten minutes with salt and pepper.

Chop up a butternut squash – you don't even need to skin it, just take out the seeds – and put the squash in the pan, along with some nice chicken stock.

Cook for thirty minutes and then purée it.

Slice some ciabatta or other good white bread and drizzle the slices with olive oil; then sprinkle lots of Parmesan on them. Fry on both sides in a non-stick frying pan with no oil.

When you serve the soup, scatter the sage leaves on top. Jamie suggests olive oil too, but – even though it's a bit of a competing (and incredibly expensive) flavour – it's hard to resist a few drops of truffle oil.

A plain green salad is good with the omelette and soup.

You're going to have to take a nap after you've finished this lunch. A happy nap.

18

On the afternoon, twelve days later, that the nurse from the clinic was due to call with the result of the pregnancy test, I decided to recruit all the help we could find. 'I'm going to walk down to the church on Quex Road and ask Mum for help,' I told Pernilla.

'Oh,' she said. 'Really? To the church?'

She came with me. It was the first time we had been inside the church, or any church, since my mother's funeral. There was a service on and we didn't stay long. I lit a candle, asked a statue of the Virgin Mary to help make Pernilla a mother, and left.

The nurse called when we got home. The test was inconclusive but not promising. Pernilla went in for another test, and the next day the nurse called again. Pernilla was not pregnant.

Something wonderful happened on that evening of limitless emptiness. In a single phone conversation, I was suddenly made free to stay at home and to cook as much as I wanted. From that moment on, wars and flights to the shit-holes where wars tend to occur would get in the way of cooking only if I wanted them to. The phone conversation was with the editor of the newspaper I had worked at for thirteen years. He told me that he would likely be asking me to move back to Long Island within months. He knew that I would decline to leave London and that this would mean I would leave the paper. Other than cleaning toilets and clearing restaurant tables, I had never had another job. The job had shaped my life for over a decade and I had adored it. I loved it and the newspaper so much that I had often put my life on the line for it. But lately I had found my job to be a yoke. Newspapers were in crisis. Local news was the only possible saviour of most American newspapers, the people who ran newspapers had decided. Foreign news in the paper would be picked up from wire services. The editor said he was sorry. But he had nothing to apologize for.

And so I became free to ramp up the search for memory traces of my mother, free to stare at the green shoots of vegetables I had planted in the garden and free to spend the mornings planning what I would cook in the afternoons. I would try to make a living from freelance writing, and if I failed, then I would look for a job.

I rented a car and two days later Pernilla and I were in Ardnamurchan, where we walked and cooked and barely ever talked about the baby we had not managed to kick-start.

A morning story at Port an Droighionn

19

There is no need for Elizabeth David's or anyone else's cookery books in the kitchen at Port an Droighionn. The cooking there is very basic. My mother shares some of the challenges faced by British women after the Second World War; the west coast in the early 1970s is not a place where garlic and olive oil are to be easily found. So tins of Spam, baked beans, tomatoes, sweetcorn, peas, haricot beans and any other kind of meat and vegetables my parents can find in the supermarket two hours' drive away mount up on the shelves.

Anything in a tin or a jar or anything dried and non-perishable is stockpiled. Anything fresh is cooked and eaten fast. My mother's other challenge is like Elizabeth David's in her dark flat next to the Nile in Cairo during the war, towards the end of her years as a refugee and junior official in the British government's centre of operations in the Middle East. Elizabeth David roasted in a metal box, made her sauces and sautéed her vegetables on two gas rings and grilled her kebabs on a portable barbecue that her beloved Sudanese servant and co-conspirator in the kitchen, Suleiman, carried on to the balcony when it filled the tiny, dark flat with smoke. My mother has two gas rings fuelled by an orange canister that leans against the house outside the kitchen and an outdoor barbecue that my father built from stones and a metal grille. And she has the Esse.

With no electricity, a solid-fuel stove is the only option. The hulking white-painted metal Esse – a pygmy Aga, really

– squats along a wall in the kitchen, hungry for coal and spewing smoke out of a chimney and, often, into the house. Coal is the dirtiest fuel, and once a week my father spends two hours on his knees, raking and gouging, cleaning the innards of the Esse. My sister and I keep out of the way when it is cleaning day.

The Esse has two settings: incredibly hot and so tepid it may as well be off. On the 'incredibly hot' setting of the Esse, my mother tries out a traditional Scottish recipe that requires just such a flat, hot metal surface as the 'girdle' – the Scots dialect name for griddle – on the top of the Esse. Drop scones are little pancakes made from a batter of self-raising flour, golden syrup, salt, milk or buttermilk, sugar and eggs. She stands in the warmth of the kitchen and mixes the ingredients in a ceramic bowl until it forms a light-yellow batter. The coal in the Esse has made the girdle so hot that a drop of water sizzles into nothing in a panicked instant. She lightly butters the girdle and immediately starts to drop the batter on to the surface from a tablespoon. The drop scones form in rounds, a dozen of them fitting on the girdle at once. She watches the batter on the upper side begin to bubble slightly and then she flips them over. The sweet warm smell fills the kitchen. When the drop scones are done, she piles them up on a plate, in a tea towel, and covers the pile to keep them warm.

She reaches for the brass bell with the black handle that sits always on a side table in the kitchen, walks out of the house and on to the slight hill behind the house, where the single, weather-beaten hawthorn tree clings on against the Atlantic winds. She rings the bell, and the noise carries across the hills and the bog to wherever we are.

Jane and I are on the sandy beach over the hill, in Swordle Bay, playing in a rock formation we have decided is our house. We grab our plastic buckets and spades and run across the sand, through the rushing waters of the Swordle Burn and up through the bracken and heather, over the dry-stone wall and

111

down the other side of the hill to our house. We know that there must be something good on the kitchen table.

We spoon honey and jam on to the warm drop scones and eat dozens, until we can eat no more.

With the supermarket so far away, finding fresh food in Ardnamurchan is a problem.

My mother begins to make compost and turns the front, north-facing part of the garden into her vegetable patch. The cold and the salt and the stony ground make it tough going – lettuces don't stand a chance, nor do most things that grow above ground – but soon we are eating her carrots, radishes, potatoes and redcurrants. My mother boils the potatoes and melts knobs of butter on top of them. There aren't many of them and they're rather small, but they are the best potatoes any of us have ever tasted.

My father shoots some rabbits with his .22 rifle, and my mother roasts a couple. The gun isn't up to shooting deer, but the local farmer, Alistair, has a larger rifle. He brings over some venison. My mother grabs what she has – red wine, oil, some dried herbs – and sinks the lean flesh of the red deer stag into a deep marinade. It sits in its pot for two days before she cooks it. It is tender, gamey and extraordinarily delicious.

Alistair's sister makes some black pudding, and even my father, a fan of black pudding, finds it a little too rich and bloody.

The sea is more bountiful than the land. We collect huge mussels from the bay, and my mother scrubs them and makes moules marinières as Elizabeth David has taught her. My parents befriend the owners of the local wild salmon fishery, and there is a ready supply of the world's best salmon, fresh and smoked. Andrew, the slightly unpredictable man who dynamited and dug our road, has failed at his house-building business and has turned to diving for scallops. He comes down to the house one day with a whole sack of the maroon and white and dun half-moon shells, and my parents pick out which ones they want. My mother prises them open at the fan end of the shell with a table knife and a spoon, running the knife along the inside of the flat side of the shell. She takes the spoon and scoops out the flesh, separating the white scallop meat from the bitter skirt that surrounds it. My father lingers over the stove as she fries them in butter. They turn the shells into ashtrays and mouse-poison holders.

We have a white fibreglass and wood dinghy with an outboard engine and a couple of oars. My father buys three second-hand lobster creels connected on a rope that ends with a pink buoy. We push quite far out into the sea when the weather is good and unfurl from spindles fishing lines of about eight hooks, with white and coloured feathers bound next to them. These are mackerel lines. A few circular lead weights tied to the end take a line to the seabed. When we feel the line go slack, we rewind the spindle several turns so that the hooks float a few feet above the bottom, invisible to us. We pull the lines up and down with one hand, smoothly, holding the spool with the other hand just in case something tugs suddenly and powerfully at the nylon twine. When a mackerel takes a hook, the line quivers; then it begins to scythe across the surface. My father teaches us to control our excitement a little bit and to stay seated where we are, so that we don't all end up in the Atlantic. There is no standing up in the boat – ever. There is no moving from your seat without permission. There is no wearing Wellington boots, which could pull us to the bottom of the sea.

One afternoon in the summer of 1976 we are motoring back along the coast towards our bay when Jane points to the port side of the boat.

'What's that?' she asks.

There is a very large fin sticking out of the water, moving slowly towards the dinghy. None of us has seen *Jaws* but since its release earlier in the year we have all been aware, like nearly everyone else on the planet, of the huge shark that terrorizes a seaside town and rips into boats, eating the people inside.

'That's a shark,' my father says in a sprightly, jaunty tone, as if he were pointing out a newborn lamb in a field. 'But I'm sure it's a basking shark and they don't have any teeth.'

'What do they eat?' I ask.

'Plankton,' my mother says. 'They just suck in these tiny, tiny little sea creatures.'

The fin moves closer.

'We should have a harpoon mounted on the boat,' my father jokes, in that excessively, suspiciously cheery voice again.

'So it can't hurt us?' Jane asks.

'The only thing basking sharks ever do is accidentally turn boats over,' my father says. 'With their tails.'

The shark is now visible. It is very big. Much bigger than the boat. It passes by. My father continues to make jokes until we are back on land. We don't go out in the boat for a few days.

Occasionally, brilliantly, when we are fishing in the boat, there are silver flashes darting around on all eight hooks in the darkness of the water as we wind in the lines, turn by turn on the spool. I learn to thwack the heads of the fish on the wooden bench in the boat, dumping them on to the bloody hull when they're dead. I'm allowed a knife, and when we get to shore I slice off the heads, slit their bellies from the anus to the neck, and pull out the guts.

My mother fries them. And, in a metal box she has bought for the purpose, she smokes the rest. There are often too many to eat fresh.

Some of the fish become bait for the creels, stuffed raw into little pouches inside the traps of netting and rusty, heavy metal frames. There are two funnel-like entrances in each creel. Lobsters are not clever enough to find their way back out.

We drop the creels from the boat into the sea about fifty yards off the rocks and leave them there for two or three days. I look at the pink buoy from the shore, wondering what's happening down below the waves. Hauling them out of the sea after a couple of days is thrilling. Each yard of rope my father pulls into the boat brings the creels closer. The first one forms a vague smudge of paleness in the water, and slowly it comes more into focus. To counterbalance the tug of the creels, either my sister or I have to sit on the other side of the boat. It is agonizing for the one whose turn it is to miss the emergence of the lobster pots, as we call them. Sometimes there is disappointment: the creels are empty. But sometimes my father lifts them into the boat, dripping with cold seawater and smelling of something alive. That means they are holding treasure. Huge hermit crabs hiding in their borrowed, barnacled shells; purple starfish spreading their sucking tentacles across the netting; spiky sea urchins my sister and I keep and then drown in fresh water so that we can make decorations out of their shells; once, a brindled dogfish, whose fin cuts through the salty water in our bathtub for an hour and who makes its escape into the bay only because my mother, the judge and executioner, decides it won't taste very good; a huge conger eel, as thick as my father's arm, its sharp teeth a horror from the depths.

'Look at that,' my father says, pointing to the eel's mouth. 'Nasty.'

'Where do they live?' I ask nervously.

'Between the rocks on the bottom, I think,' my father says.

The conger goes the way of the dogfish, slithering out of the creel into the rocks in the bay when we return to shore. For years afterwards I expect it to bite me as I swim over those rocks at high tide.

But the crabs and the lobsters are the gems. My mother drops them into pans of boiling water, the deep-blue lobsters squealing and turning instantly pink. When they're done, she dresses the lobsters with mayonnaise and sits at the white Formica table cracking open the huge crabs, scooping out the edible meat, discarding the rest, and refilling the shells the size of my father's hand with all the good bits.

At the end of one summer, a local farmer sells us two sheep, gutted and headless.

'This is not strictly legal,' my father explains to Jane and me, smiling as he wraps the two carcasses in black rubbish bags and straps them to the roof of the car. Slaughtering and selling whole sheep is against governmental health guidelines. The farmer is extremely keen that our cargo escape the notice of the police. It is a five-hour drive to Edinburgh and we have a full car, our yellow Vauxhall estate. There is only the one, single-track road out of Ardnamurchan, and along the way we will have to drive past the tiny police station in a small town named Strontian, where in 1798 strontium was discovered in a lead mine in the hills. We will not be stopping in the public toilets in Strontian. Sometimes the region's only policeman is encountered along the road. We will have to take our chances.

As we wind our way along the road, we can hear the flapping plastic on the roof. We make baaing sounds and joke about being arrested as McAllester sheep stealers, and my father retells a nonsense story about the unusual spelling of our last name that his father used to tell him when he was a boy: the McAllisters were sheep stealers, and one day they were found out, their dastardly crimes exposed. 'So they slipped away and, in a moment of cunning and wile, they changed the "i" in McAllister to an "e" and escaped detection for ever,' my father says.

We, too, escape detection, and two hours after setting off down the single-track road we make it to the Corran Ferry, where we have to queue for the boat to take us across the sea loch to where the road opens up to two lanes and heads south towards Glasgow and Edinburgh. We get out of the car to inspect the sheep on the roof. Their raw legs have torn through the black plastic and stick upward. They are very obviously the legs of two dead sheep. A couple of pools of blood form on the yellow-painted roof. The four of us look at one another with silent, laughing faces, not meeting the eyes of the other people waiting for the ferry.

We eat mutton in Edinburgh, every way my mother can think of cooking it, for weeks afterwards.

∽

Drop Scones

I found this recipe in Theodora Fitzgibbon's *A Taste of Scotland*, another of my mother's cookery books.

You don't need a griddle, really. A large, heavy frying pan will do.

For two dozen little pancakes, mix up four cups (American-sized cups, but a normal teacup or mug will do) of self-raising flour, three heaped tablespoons of sugar, a pinch of salt and two tablespoons of warmed golden syrup. Then add half a pint of milk or buttermilk and two beaten eggs. Mix everything together until you have a smooth batter. Heat a griddle or pan hot enough to make a drop of water dance, butter lightly, and start spooning out the batter on to the hot surface. Flip the scones over when they begin to bubble.

They are best eaten immediately, hot and delicious, spread with butter and honey. So try to call people into the kitchen either just before or while you're making the drop scones.

Fishing on a cold day in Ardnamurchan

20

Before it was time to load up on drugs and hormones for the second try at IVF, Pernilla went to Vancouver to visit her family. I cooked. And for the first time in a decade, I knew that no matter what happened in the world, I would not be disturbed by a phone call that would send me racing to the airport.

It was midsummer, and the food available in the farmers' markets just seemed to be happy food. The garlic was green and fresh from the ground, mild enough so that a whole bulb could be chopped and fried like an onion. The green-topped carrots made a loud snapping noise when you bit into them. And the berries began to pile up on the tables at our local farmers' market and at the stalls on the pavement outside our nearest Tube station.

There is no happier food I can think of than the strawberry. It is not as challenging as the gooseberry or as special as the raspberry, perhaps, but I think strawberries make people smile more than just about any food I can think of.

I stood at one of the stands at the farmers' market in Queen's Park, staring at the boxes of strawberries. I had brought two big shopping bags. But how many? I bought twenty-five pounds of strawberries and walked up the hill, pink juice beginning to drip happily on to the pavement.

In my memory, nothing in my mother's food output had been more special than strawberry ice cream.

*   *   *

I come home after school on a summer evening: 'We're going to get the strawberries tomorrow, aren't we, Mum?' I ask.

'Yes,' she says quickly, 'don't worry.'

In the morning we set off in the yellow Vauxhall for the farm outside Edinburgh. I love this annual expedition.

There's a sign at the turn-off saying: 'Pick Your Own Strawberries'.

'Can we pick our own?' I ask, imagining the opportunities for eating as I pick.

'No, we're just buying them,' my mother says.

'Please.'

'No.'

We arrive at the farm, and she buys more strawberries than I can believe. We place the punnets of berries in the boot in a tight fit, and still some have to sit on top of the others. The berries bleed into the soft green cardboard of the punnets, and I lean over from the back seat all the way home, picking out the hugest strawberries I can find.

Three things can happen to them. An almost unlimited supply is immediately made available for eating. We eat them plain, with cream, and with vanilla ice cream after lunch, for a teatime snack, after dinner, and during the Wimbledon men's singles final the next day as my hero, Björn Borg, is given a fright on his way to his fifth successive Wimbledon title by the snarly, spoiled American kid with the ugly curly hair and the terrifyingly angled serve.

My mother takes a second batch of strawberries and weighs them carefully. She reaches into a cabinet and takes out a huge aluminium pan with a loose, curved handle – like a cauldron's. She tips the strawberries into the pan and adds a cascade of white sugar. As the house begins to smell of boiling, bubbling, breaking-down strawberries, she lines up the jars she has collected and writes on labels with a green Pentel pen in her jagged script: 'Strawberry'. When the jam is ready, she pours it into the jars and quickly places a disc of greaseproof paper on the surface of the jam before sealing it all with an elastic band snapped over a transparent, deliberately too-large square of plastic she has cut out. I will eat this jam on toast all through the winter, and for all my father's and sister's insistence that, really, raspberry jam is the best jam, I never tire of strawberry.

But what I hanker for most of all is the ice cream, to which I hope a third batch of strawberries will be dedicated. She makes it only rarely. If she makes it, it fills only one plastic container. It is the most intense and delicious flavour I have ever experienced.

'Make the ice cream, Mum,' I beg. 'Please.'

'But it's a lot of work. I'm tired.'

This time she makes it.

And now, more than twenty-five years later, I wanted to taste it again. I felt sure there would be, within her own recipe book, a handwritten description of how to concoct this most strawberry-ish of strawberry ice creams. Written down decades before, like the directions to the buried treasure. For the first time in months, I opened a book that still seemed almost too electric with memory and emotion to touch.

There was nothing there of any help at all. No mention of strawberry ice cream in her hand. Or any ice cream.

'You're not playing along with this, Mum,' I said out loud.

There were no recipes for strawberry ice cream in *French Country Cooking* or even the massive *French Provincial Cooking*. I picked up the *Observer* magazine and flicked through it. And there, as if sent from above, was a recipe for strawberry ice cream. OK, it wasn't from Elizabeth David or Katie Stewart or Robert Carrier. It was written by the popular British cookery book writer Nigel Slater. But in the family tree of cookery book writers and chefs, Nigel Slater is only one or two branches away from Elizabeth David. As is just about every chef working in Britain and most in the United States. Alice

122

Waters, perhaps the most influential chef in the United States, sat down as a young woman, read *French Provincial Cooking* from cover to cover and, to grossly oversimplify the story of her myriad influences, thus embarked on the journey to her doctrine of seasonal, simple, Mediterranean-inspired, local-produce-filled cooking. Alice and Liz became dear friends. The legacy spreads deeply into American and British restaurants and cookery books. The River Café, perhaps London's loveliest restaurant, thrives off Elizabeth David's obsessions with seasonality, simplicity, local produce, the Mediterranean and just having an incredibly great time over food and wine. The restaurant's alumni include more brilliant cooks – Sam and Sam Clark of my favourite restaurant in the world, Moro; the seasonally obsessed TV chef, Hugh Fearnley-Whittingstall; and Jamie Oliver.

They are all Elizabeth David's children, or grandchildren, really. When not directly stealing her recipes, as Fearnley-Whittingstall does with her brilliant French onion tart, they are borrowing heavily, fifty years after she first published.

So I looked at Nigel Slater's recipe for strawberry ice cream, and its simplicity and loveliness seemed to speak of a history that stretched back to the imperious Mrs David and from her to one of her devoted followers – my mother. 'The simplest and best', Slater began. It had only three ingredients. One pound of strawberries. Three and a half ounces of baker's sugar. Ten fluid ounces of heavy cream. After removing the leaves, slice the strawberries. Cover them in the sugar for an hour, macerating. Whip up the cream, 'thick enough to lie in folds rather than stiff enough to stand in peaks'. Zap the strawberries in a blender. Fold it all together, leaving a bit of a ripple. Cover and freeze. 'It is worth checking and stirring the ice as it freezes, bringing the outside edges into the middle.'

I did as he said. I took out the blue plastic bowl from the freezer four hours later and left it to soften a little for twenty minutes. It was a thick swirl of pink and pinker. I took my first bite. The coldness filled my mouth, followed a moment later by a sort of warmth, the warmth of a flavour mixing with memory and love. The intense strawberryness made me see the plastic, shop-bought ice cream container – Wall's vanilla – my mother had kept and then filled with her strawberry ice cream.

Her elbow bends as she digs into it with a strong silvery spoon, scooping out chunks into bowls in front of my sister and me. We are forbidden to help ourselves, because my mother knows there will be none left within minutes.

And the present and the past blended for me. I closed my eyes in the kitchen and I imagined my mother somewhere, smiling at my childlike grin, the gift of strawberry joy successfully passed down from the dead to the living.

She had more to bestow. I stood on a chair and lifted down her old aluminium jam dish, or preserving pan: slightly misshapen, alarmingly big, built solely for the purpose of boiling fruit. I remembered it sitting on my mother's stove, bubbling and steaming, vapours of impossible sweetness snaking their way out and filling the house.

'Do not get too close to it,' she warns me. I stand on a wooden stool five feet away and peer into the dark, simmering gloop inside, slightly afraid and entirely desperate to stick my finger into it. She picks up the wooden spoon with the extra-long handle that rests next to the stove on the worktop and dips it into the pan. She blows on the runny jam until it's cooled and thickened a little, and she steers it into my open mouth.

Elizabeth David wrote an entire – and very long – book about bread, but from what I could tell she wasn't overly interested in jam. There was, again, nothing in my mother's own recipe book. So I looked on my shelves and found another book of hers, one I had never looked at: *The Penguin Book of Jams, Pickles and Chutneys,* by David and Rose Mabey, some of its pages stuck together in a corner with big splotches of darkness. Strawberry jam got two whole pages to itself. Katie Stewart offered a slight alternative, with a shorter recipe. I began to read, expecting the revelation of an alchemy. But making jam turned out to be about as difficult as boiling the kettle. Which makes you wonder why on earth anyone buys jam from a shop.

I dumped strawberries, sugar and the juice of two lemons into the huge pan and turned on the heat. Not very long after that I had enough strawberry jam, albeit ridiculously runny – 'Ah, so that's what a "setting point" is,' I said when my sister asked how long I had boiled the jam – to keep Pernilla and me alive during the winter. I went quickly back to the market and bought raspberries and filled some more jars with a darker jam. I lined them up on the kitchen table, all labelled and covered with transparent plastic discs and elastic bands.

21

My sister and I are running along the beach at Gullane in East Lothian, outside Edinburgh, after a Sunday lunch of roast pork with apple sauce. In the car home we are tired and floppy, made perfectly content by the ritual visit to the world's best ice cream shop – Luca's in Musselburgh. Here Jane has once again broken her own world record for the slowest consumption of an ice cream, the tip of her tongue dabbing tormentingly at the pink-and-white swirl.

Mine was long gone by the time she was halfway through her pointillist approach to eating.

Now we sit in the white enamel bath in our flat on Oxford Terrace and squirt water at each other through empty shampoo bottles.

'Time to wash your hair,' my mother says. She is sitting on the closed toilet, smoking a cigarette.

'Can you get Daddy, please?' I ask. We all know the drill. I will not let my mother wash my hair, because only my father knows how to do it without getting soapy water in my eyes. And he must use the same handleless, transparent, slightly grey-coloured plastic cup each time. This is one of the logic-free demands a child will make that his parents realize is, in the end, better to surrender to. Jane washes her own hair and gets out of the bath. My father comes in and gently pours warm water over my scalp with one hand, using his other as a dam across my tilted forehead. Just in case. He massages in the shampoo and rinses my hair after he has placed his hand-dam back on my forehead.

'Can we have a funny supper, Mummy?' I hear Jane ask in the kitchen. Sunday could be about to get even better. A funny supper on a Sunday is pretty common but by no means guaranteed. And it brings with it the added benefit of taking place in front of the television. I stop splashing to listen.

'OK,' my mother says.

This is very good news. And soon I can smell the cold roasted potatoes, which we call crispity potatoes, being sautéed in the kitchen. There will also be cold roast pork and apple sauce, but beyond that I don't know what's coming. It's part of the excitement. The plate just arrives. Although it is possible, within the unwritten rules of the funny supper, to lobby gently for constituent parts. A piece of celery. Potato crisps with ketchup to dip into. Pickled onions. A chunk of cheddar. Sausages. Tomatoes with mayonnaise on the side. Peanuts. Chocolate fingers, whose chocolate you can suck or lick off, leaving the boring biscuit exposed. Carrot sticks. Slices of salami. Coleslaw. Crackers. Slices of cucumber. Ham. Grilled cheese on toast with Lea & Perrins nearby. An apple. Warmed-up vegetables from lunch. Chocolate-covered digestive biscuits. Sometimes, when there are no roast potatoes left from lunch, my mother pulls out her chip pan, already full of pre-used vegetable oil, and starts peeling and slicing up potatoes into chips. Somewhere in the mass of chips will sometimes be a surprise M, a J, a D and another M. Matt, Jane, Dad, Mum. That means Dad has been in the kitchen to do a little potato sculpting.

(One autumn we have an American philosophy student lodging with us, a warm, cheery kid named Dirk who teaches me how to spin my football on one finger as, he explains, basketball players do. If Dirk is at home when chips are on the menu, my father carves out another D. Dirk loves chips almost as much as I do, and one night he takes me out to the chip shop with his drawling, hairy college buddies, all on their semester abroad, and we sit on a public bench eating chips and drinking Coke, which he has bought. On the evening before Dirk returns home to West Virginia and leaves a hole in the family, my father presents him with a gift he has been making, secretly, in his workshop downstairs; a gold-sprayed chip made of perfectly carved wood, pierced by a real fork, with a glass drip about to plop down from the chip. It is on a small plinth.)

I sit on the floor in my pyjamas, cross-legged under the square coffee table with the white Formica top. My sister sits beside me in her nightgown. The Sony television is on. Mum comes in carrying two plates. I sit up as tall as I can to see what's on them.

22

In vitro fertilization often requires a woman to take lots of hormones and drugs whose names are hard to keep track of if you're not personally taking them but whose effects seem to be, more or less, universal. Most of them are delivered through needles, several times a day; some of the needles are very large indeed. At times, this combination can make the woman in question a little moody. One day during our second attempt to make a baby in a Petri dish, I showed my wife a couple of Internet videos that I had found amusing and hoped would make her laugh: thousands of Filipino prisoners in orange jumpsuits perfectly recreating the videos to Michael Jackson's 'Thriller' and Queen's 'Radio Ga Ga'. Pernilla watched, and when Freddie Mercury sang, 'Someone still loves you', in 'Radio Ga Ga', tears began to trickle down her cheeks. They were not tears of laughter.

'It's so sad,' she said.

'What? It's hilarious,' I said.

'But they're all locked up,' she said. 'There's no one to look after them.'

'You're so sweet,' I said.

Which was the wrong thing to say.

'Why, because I'm all hormonal and find it sad that there are all these prisoners and I cry when they sing, "Someone still loves you", and I think that perhaps they're there in prison in the Philippines and no one loves them, no one even fucking knows they're there?'

For all her mood swings as her body went through the extreme pushings and pullings of vast amounts of drugs and hormones for the second time in only a few months, Pernilla remained the person in the world who made me happiest. The doctors said that she had probably been pregnant briefly the first time – hence the confused reading – and so we had quickly gone for another cycle of IVF. I fed her obsessively. If the embryologist had his sums right, 9 August was the day that one or both of the two embryos implanted inside Pernilla would embed itself in the lining of her uterus. She would, at that point, be pregnant.

That day I woke up absolutely certain that we were about to become expectant parents. As I ran in Queen's Park that morning I pictured myself introducing my daughter or son to some of life's treats, as my mother had done for me.

It is a Saturday morning and I am sitting cross-legged in our playroom, staring at the Sony Trinitron television. There is a black-and-white film on starring a young man with black hair. He hits someone in a bar and ends up in prison. I sense that his fate is unfair and I feel terrible for him. But then things get better in prison. He makes friends and, before long, they're singing and dancing to the most amazing music I have ever heard.

I run upstairs to the kitchen when the movie ends.

'Mum, do you have any records by Elvis Presley?'

'No, darling,' she says. 'I don't think so. But look through the records.'

It's as though I'm famished. I run through to the living room and riffle through the LPs, but all I can find is classical, jazz, a couple of Simon & Garfunkels, Judy Collins, Joan Armatrading, Harry Nilsson, the Kingston Trio, Mozart, Beethoven and other records by other people I don't care about. I want Elvis, and I cannot believe that my mother and father have none of his records. Specifically, the record.

'But isn't "Jailhouse Rock" the best song ever made?' I ask, slightly desperate now, searching for confirmation to what I see as a self-evident truth. 'It must have sold millions of copies. How come you don't have one?'

'I was never really that keen on Elvis,' she says, and I look at her in amazement. 'But why don't you buy it with your birthday money?'

This is perhaps the cleverest thing my mother has ever suggested, I decide. Granny and Grandpa McAllester send me a crisp new pound every year in an envelope. I keep it safely in a brass box with a key until I find just the right thing to spend it on. Sweets, in other words. I have never bought or owned a record before.

We drive through the Robert Adam-designed New Town of Edinburgh, one of the most beautiful sections of any city in the world, but I don't see it. I don't see anything. I only hear a noise – the sound of Elvis in my head. We park as close as possible to John Menzies, a big stationer that also sells books and records. We rush up to the floor where the records are. I'm planning to ask them to play it for me, just to make sure it's the same as the song I heard in the movie.

'Have you got your pound?' my mother says. 'Let's go to the forty-fives.'

Under 'P' we find no Elvis singles. This is a mistake, surely. How could they not have numerous copies of the best song ever made?

'Let's go and ask,' my mother says. She squeezes my hand.

We approach the desk.

'Do you have "Jailhouse Rock" by Elvis Presley?' I ask the young woman behind the counter.

'Hang on,' she says, turning round to look through the racks of singles. She turns back. 'No, sorry, but it might be on an album.'

We look under 'P' and find a selection of Christmas songs sung by Elvis, although he doesn't look much like the sleek young man I saw in the movie. He looks big, and his hair is bigger.

'Let's see if they can order it,' my mother says.

'Can I order "Jailhouse Rock", please?' I ask the young woman behind the counter.

She takes out a big book and flicks through it.

'Sorry, they don't make singles of "Jailhouse Rock" any more,' she says.

My mother drives home and I sit in front of the record player for an hour. I am desolate and, more to the point, newly aware that the world is not what I expected it to be.

'Matty, come in here,' my mother calls out.

I go into the kitchen and she is melting what she calls 'cooking chocolate' – in other words, it's good when it's in a chocolate crispy but kind of horrible when eaten in chunks – in a bowl that sits in a pan of hot water. A box of corn-flakes sits next to the cooker. She has already positioned a tall wooden stool beside her. I leap on to it and stare at the chunks of chocolate as they disappear into the goo that's beginning to collect at the bottom of the bowl. The kitchen is filled with wafts of warm cocoa. She takes her spatula, and her wrist turns clockwise as the melted chocolate pours into the mixing bowl where she has put the cornflakes. Then she places the bowl that held the chocolate on the kitchen worktop next to me.

'Go on then,' she says, smiling. And my index finger slides its way around the sides of the bowl and into my mouth, and rock 'n' roll records can wait.

23

When I got home from my run on 9 August, I found an email from my father, who had just spent several days in Ardnamurchan with my sister. 'Jane has some info for you,' he wrote.

My sister called when she reached London.

'What's the info?' I said.

She had told our father about her trips to the church on Farm Street, how she lit candles for our mother in the small chapel to Our Lady of Lourdes and how she felt close to our mother there for some reason.

'Yes,' I said, having heard this before. I was still not terribly interested in churches, especially ones that I had never been to.

'Well,' my sister went on, 'Dad said to me: "You know, Matt was christened in that church." '

And I felt another connection made – small and meaningless perhaps, rooted in a religion I did not share, but the past felt like a slightly less intimidating thing to me.

Father Joseph Christie, Jesuit priest and sometime television and radio personality, is waiting for my father in a gloomy little room in the church on Farm Street. My father is twenty-four, an atheist from a Protestant family wanting to marry a Catholic. That means he has to learn the ropes of the Church. My mother's father lines up ten sessions with the priest for his future son-in-law.

Christie is about five foot ten, stocky, good-looking and as sharp as a whip. He waits for my father in the ground-floor room. It is empty but for a table and two chairs. There is one window. My father decides that this room is set aside for lessons like those to which he has committed himself. It is an island of monastical asceticism in a building bubbling over with shimmering gold leaf, marble statues of the Virgin, mosaics of cobalt and crimson, all of it surrounded by the impossible wealth of Mayfair.

My father is still a student of photography and living in London without my mother. She is in Edinburgh, where they met while at university. An arts degree was not for him, he decided quickly, and he moved to London to study photography. But he's very much in love with the young woman he met in a coffee bar one day. Her name is Ann Taylor.

He drives to church in his light-blue Sunbeam Alpine sports car after classes finish. It is early summer and London is at its best.

'Donald, I'd like you to take these away and read them before next time,' Christie says at the end of the first session, handing my father a bundle of pamphlets. 'I want you to fire some questions at me next time.'

My father likes the priest enormously and enjoys the first forty-five-minute session. Christie is fiercely intelligent, and my father feels intellectually exercised as he zips up Park Lane after the meeting, with the car's top down in the evening sunshine. He does his homework and the classes continue. The day before the fourth session with Christie, something in one of the pamphlets catches my father's eye.

'OK,' my father, the would-be husband, says when they meet at the church. 'What about the Catholic teaching in relation to the situation when a mother's life is threatened by the birth of a child? As I understand it, the teaching says that the child is more important and that the mother would therefore die. How on earth can you justify that?'

134

'You see, Donald, these days the advances in modern medicine are so great that this situation never arises,' the priest says, looking uncomfortable.

'But that's not always been the case and it's not the case in many countries. And besides, it's the teaching I find troubling.'

'As I said, Donald,' Christie says, 'this situation never arises these days.'

At the end of that session, Christie pronounces that my father has learned enough and there is no need for the next six lessons.

He wishes my father all the best in his marriage.

Six years later my mother gives birth to me, her second child.

She chooses the Farm Street church as the site of my christening. It is 16 December 1969. Afterwards, the families go to our house for tea. I am dressed in a very long white christening robe. My mother poses for pictures with me, holding me on her lap with one hand, smoking a cigarette with the other.

24

Pernilla and I sat watching crap television shows on a weekday afternoon when we should both have been working. We were waiting for a phone call from the IVF clinic. I had refused to believe that this time it would be anything but successful. I only wondered whether we would have a boy, a girl, or twins. Besides cooking and jabbing Pernilla in the bottom each morning with a needle the size of a pencil lead, my only job throughout the IVF was to be cheery. The night before I had not felt very cheery all of a sudden, and I dreamed about the test results all night. The phone rang.

'Oh, no, not again,' Pernilla said, her face crumpling.

The test results were inconclusive but not promising. Pernilla would have to do another blood test the next day. I called the nurse back. 'It's fifty–fifty,' she said. I stared out the window at nothing.

Our favourite restaurant, Moro, called to confirm our booking. I had planned a celebration. 'Actually, I was just going to call you to cancel,' I said.

There was little to be done in the way of cooking, making jokes, cheering each other up, discussing how we felt, or even talking. I went to my study and closed the door and cried. I wanted to buy a first record for someone. I wanted to sit on the rocks in Ardnamurchan with my arms around someone small and tell him or her that I would dive in without a second's hesitation. I wanted to make one beautiful, delicious, special meal after another for my family. I wanted someone to be alive who was not alive. Not my mother this time, but a child. I would be the one doing the looking after. I'd be doing the parenting and I'd make sure that I'd do it well, for the rest of my life, not just until the little person was about ten years old. I would not disappear into madness and drinking.

But on this day it had all begun to seem as impossible as bringing my mother back.

The next days became all about the amount of hCG, or human chorionic gonadotropin, detectable in Pernilla's blood. This is a hormone created by the cells that form the placenta, which is the root of nourishment for a growing embryo. (I liked to picture the placenta as a French country dining table laden with fresh, colourful, delicious food with only one place setting – for a ravenous, growing embryo.) The level of hCG in Pernilla's blood would hopefully at least double every two days. If it didn't, the embryo would be giving up the ghost. Currently, it was on 15. A reading of 25 or more is considered a positive pregnancy.

I forced myself up to the kitchen, wanting to find some comfort there. An unprompted memory surfaced, of my mother's thick, yeasty home-made bread. I poured some wholemeal flour, yeast and water into a bowl and pounded the dough with my fists.

My mother stands next to me in the kitchen in Edinburgh, showing me how to use my upper-body weight to lean into the warm sticky mixture, pushing it away from me in a kind of rocking motion across the flour she has scattered on the Formica worktop. She picks it up and slaps it down on the surface and I do the same, louder and harder. The house fills with the oven-rich smell of fresh bread baking.

The phone rang again. It was the doctor. The team of doctors at the clinic had looked at the blood-test results and they'd decided that the embryo, giving off an hCG reading of 15, had a chance.

Pernilla and I had been calling the embryo Bongo. Bongo was there inside her, but he was weak. Pernilla had a whole ream of new instructions – inject more of this, stop that, get up at the crack of dawn and come straight to the clinic because you'll probably be on a plasma drip all day.

'It's the Battle for Bongo,' I said, and we smiled and I went into the kitchen on my own, closed the door and gave the risen dough an even harder pounding. Then I soaked some dried porcini mushrooms, sliced up some prosciutto and some garlic, and made a creamy, peppery pasta sauce.

We were up just after dawn and driving to the clinic. Pernilla gave more blood. The embryo had not given up; the hCG level was now at 24.

'Sorry, but does that mean she's pregnant?' I asked the doctor, a quiet man who spoke in a mumble.

'Yes,' he said, smiling in a sort of regretful way, 'but it's an embryo that's trying to get by.'

The doctor said the clinic would be monitoring Pernilla and the embryo carefully over the coming days. But the bottom line was this: it might well be abnormal. Poor. Doomed. Or it could be just behind schedule and a bit weak right now.

'If it does survive, when will we know that it's going to be OK?' I asked.

'To be honest, in twelve weeks,' he said.

If Bongo was abnormal, there was fuck all I could do about it, I thought, as I drove home quickly so that I could jab my newly pregnant wife, who was sitting next to me, in the bottom with the elephant needle. But if he was just struggling a bit, then he could do with some good fuel.

Pernilla went to bed and I went to the kitchen to make Friday afternoon lunch. It was the first meal I was making knowing for sure that I would be feeding an embryo that had a real chance. So I took a root of horseradish out of the fridge and pared it down, grating it into a bowl and mixing it with vinegar, English mustard, salt and sugar. 'You're totally going to like this,' I said to the embryo. 'Just a taste of what's to come over the years ahead.'

I added yogurt to the horseradish mixture (it should really have been crème fraîche, but I didn't have any) and put a very small joint of beef in the oven, alongside the loaf that I had left to rise overnight. I boiled some carrots in a little water, a lot of butter, some sugar and a pinch of salt and reduced the mixture until there was a sweet, delicious glaze all over the crispy carrots.

'I'm getting the impression that you're cooking away your stress,' Pernilla said, when she came into the kitchen after her nap.

What I was really doing was making the only vaguely useful contribution to the embryo's survival I could think of. From now on, now that I knew he or she was in there, I'd up my game and feed Pernilla and Bongo as my mother once fed me. I planned a trip to Britain's best food market, the incredible Borough Market, for the next day. But there was somewhere else I had to stop by too.

∽

Jim Lahey's Astonishing Bread

(Via Mark Bittman and my friend Michael Schurter, and with apologies to Elizabeth David because it's better than anything she seems to have ever come up with, as far as I can tell, even though her *English Bread and Yeast Cookery* is a masterpiece.)

For some months, my friend Michael Schurter, who lives in Minneapolis, was insisting that I should try this 'no-knead' bread recipe that the *New York Times* food writer, Mark Bittman, had been touting. Bittman was given it by Jim Lahey, of the Sullivan Street Bakery in New York. I didn't see the point of bread that one didn't knead. Wasn't kneading part of the fun? On a visit to Minneapolis in the autumn of 2007, Michael made a loaf to show me what he'd been raving about. It was absolutely amazing. Since then I have made no other kind of bread. It is the one recipe in the world I feel limitlessly evangelical about. I know I'm one of many who feel that way.

I'm going to take the serious liberty of simplifying Lahey's and Bittman's recipe a bit. They include a second rising of the dough. I skip that part.

Take three (American) cups of flour and put in a mixing bowl. (One cup of flour is 110 grams of flour but the point here is proportionality, so even if you don't have American-style measuring cups, just use a normal cup or mug and use the same cup for the water measurement below.) Try white bread flour the first time because white gives the most delicious results, but you can use whatever you want.

Add a good pinch of salt, a quarter to half a teaspoon of easy yeast and stir that around.

Then add one and a half cups (or 350 ml) of water, preferably a bit tepid.

Stir the dough with a wooden spoon. This is the no-knead part. It's an unusually wet dough, so just stir it until it's all mixed up.

Cover with cling-film for between eighteen and twenty-four hours. It will look weird and glutinous and bubbly by the end.

Heat the oven to 220 centigrade and put a casserole dish with a lid – an oval Le Creuset is perfect – inside the oven to heat up until it is seriously hot.

Take it out when it's hot and sprinkle some oats or oat bran or whatever you want on the bottom of the casserole. Using your hands, lift the sticky dough out of the bowl and into the casserole. Sprinkle some white flour over the top of it.

Put the lid on and place the casserole in the oven for thirty minutes. Then take the lid off and keep it in for another fifteen minutes.

Take the casserole out and tip the loaf on to a metal cooling rack. Let it cool down a bit and then tuck in. It's miraculous. You may never buy bread again.

Homework in the kitchen at Oxford Terrace

25

As far as I know, when I visited the Farm Street church which my sister had been so strongly drawn to after my mother's death, on a Saturday morning in 2007, it was only the second time I had been there. Pernilla and I had spent a couple of hours at the glorious Borough Market, and when we drove over to the church, our old Golf was full of apples, pancetta, lardo, hard Italian cheese, a pound of freshly roasted coffee, and bags of vegetables and other cheeses and fish.

We went in through the back entrance, at the nave end, and looked up at the most beautiful church I had ever seen in London.

There was a mid-afternoon sense of quiet, the hush between services. A wedding was scheduled, but for now the church was ours.

We found the chapel my sister had told me about – Our Lady of Lourdes. Lourdes, the place of miracles. Bestowed on the visiting millions by a mother who, they say, conceived a miracle child.

(Months later, my aunt Jennifer told me that she and my mother had visited the miraculous grotto in Lourdes when they were children.)

Pernilla and I sat in the chapel of a faith neither of us believed in. I prayed. And as my sister had experienced, I felt the goodness and closeness of our mother. I sat on the bench and looked at the marble statue of Our Lady of Lourdes. Behind me were plaques embedded in the ancient walls, memorializing men who had fallen in the First World War. And there was one anonymously thanking Our Lady for 'a prayer heard and answered'.

'Is it selfish to ask for a life?' I asked the statue.

'Mum,' I said to my mother, 'you would have wanted me to have a kid, your grandchild. Do what you can, will you? Put a word in. Intercede, will you?'

'Mum,' I say to my mother, as we sit in the kitchen in Edinburgh, 'I don't understand why you pray to the Virgin Mary. She was just human. Why not pray to Jesus? Or directly to God?'

'Mary can intercede.'

'What does "intercede" mean?'

'She can put a good word in. She has a lot of influence. She's God's mummy.'

But I have my doubts. I come back from school one day a couple of years later, when I am twelve, having learned a new word.

'Mum, do you believe in transubstantiation?'

'Of course I do,' she says.

'But that means you believe that you're literally, actually, genuinely drinking blood and eating flesh when you take Communion. Right?'

'Yes,' she says.

'That's sick. You have to be joking. It's only a symbol, right?'

'If that's what you want to think, fine,' she says. 'I'll believe what I want to believe.'

I sense she's not entirely convinced by all of this. My father had promised to help bring up any children he would have with my mother as good Catholics, but it hasn't happened. There has been no First Communion, no Confirmation, no Confession. Only a bit of Sunday school, some reading of a fun, illustrated Bible full of excellent stories about lions and long hair and a sea parting and a golden statue and an old man with a big grey beard in the clouds. And the occasional trip to church. In truth, my mother has drifted from the Church and its prohibition of the Pill and other teachings she has begun to see as antediluvian. So her attempts to persuade my sister and me that God even exists become perfunctory.

'Mum,' I say, on what is perhaps our last visit together to a church, 'what's that for?' I'm bored and I've spotted a purple velvet hat-shaped thing perched on a gold-coloured stand at the front of the church.

'That's where God lives,' she whispers sharply, not encouraging further discussion. And with that sentence, she kills God off for me. God lives in a velvet hat? I don't think so. I refuse to go to church again.

Years later I realized that inside the velvet cover was the sacrament, the body and the blood of Christ.

Since the day of the velvet hat, I had lived 'as if'. As if there were a God or some kind of overarching goodness keeping things together. Not that I believed in it. It had not kept my family together. But I suspect that living 'as if' is a common trick many atheists play when the awfulness of human behaviour seems unbearable or natural disasters like tsunamis or mental illness strike without warning. Or when you are really in trouble and have no one to appeal to. Every now and then, however – and this moment in the early afternoon in the church on Farm Street was one of those times – I strayed into the slightly more theological, wishful territory of 'if'. Or 'perhaps'.

Or 'just in case'. I put my absolute disbelief to one side for a minute. And I cared nothing about the essential dishonesty of my thoughts.

The wedding was about to begin. The church was filling up with Korean Catholics. Pernilla and I left Farm Street through the back door, and on the way out I noticed on the announcement board outside what the church's proper name was: the Church of the Immaculate Conception.

* * *

The feeding blizzard was intense.

While Pernilla lay in bed, resting in the hope that the embryo inside would continue to grow, I walked to the bottom of the garden, snipped three small courgettes from the vegetable patch, and went to the kitchen to make lunch – a frittata with free-range eggs, some fresh Parmesan and lots of pepper.

For dinner that night I cooked the two line-caught sea bass we had bought at the market. I scored them twice, as Elizabeth David instructed, rubbed them with olive oil and salt, laid some fresh thyme on their sides and grilled them. (This was a mere five sentences in my recipe book but it's one of those simple, perfect, very useful things you never forget, like learning to tie a tie.) And in the days that followed, I kept on with my cooking and feeding programme. From Elizabeth David's *Italian Food* book – a miracle of research at the time of publication – I learned a good, simple way to sauté aubergines, dicing them, salting them for an hour, pouring off the muddy liquid, frying them slowly and adding garlic towards the end. From the same, a salsa verde, which I had never made before. The River Café ladies, Ruth Rogers and Rose Gray – two of the most passionate disciples of Elizabeth David's credo of simplicity and seasonality – suggested I add lots of olive oil and Parmesan to my mashed potatoes.

I shelled peas, made an intense stock with a prosciutto hock, and turned it into the River Café's pea and prosciutto soup, which we ate with slices of yeasty, home-made bread.

There were some mistakes in my flurry of chopping and shopping and roasting. Thai green curry was meant to break the Mediterranean rhythm. It was a disgusting, humiliating failure.

As was a very bad-smelling cold soup of radishes and mint.

But there was also a chorizo paella, oozing warmth and togetherness. Salads from the garden's endless supply of rocket and lettuces – and the occasional carrot, radish, spinach leaf and impossibly perfect tomato.

～

Chorizo Paella

I've adapted this from the first Moro cookery book, which is one of the two or three books I use the most – sometimes, even, without it splayed open on the table.

I know classic paella is stuffed full of seafood but this chorizo version is so delicious and cosy that you won't miss the prawns. But I also think it works really well with prawns or other seafood chucked in. You'll have to cook them briefly in the pan before you start, though, putting them on a plate to one side and throwing them back in at the last minute. The chorizo will remain the dominant taste but the prawns or squid will give a lovely extra layer to it all.

Apart from the chopping of the chorizo and vegetables, there's one bit of preparation you have to do before you start your paella. If you can, find a Spanish food shop – or website – that sells ñora peppers. They're delicious and worth tracking down, although, as the Moro people say, you can use other dried red peppers or sweet and hot paprika instead. If you've found a ñora pepper, tear it open, discard the seeds and the stalk, tear up the pepper into smallish bits and put the pieces in a little bowl of boiling water. The water softens up the flaky bits of the pepper and brings out its flavour. Half an hour is fine, an hour is better. You discard the water before you use the ñora in the paella.

To start with, slice up about three or four chorizo sausages into smallish pieces. Heat some olive oil in a broad frying pan and throw in the chorizo, soon followed by two finely chopped onions and a chopped green or red pepper. The green contrasts

148

with the slight sweetness of the chorizo, the red complements it. It's up to you.

Cook that for about fifteen to twenty minutes on a medium to low heat – don't let it dry up and don't allow the chorizo to burn – and then add a few chopped cloves of garlic. I am being deliberately vague with some of this because, as Elizabeth David taught me, it's just more fun and empowering to feel your way into a dish like paella, to make it slightly your own. You can't mess it up, really. You can only make it better with trial and error.

Let the mixture cook for a few more minutes and then add 250 g of calasparra rice, which is the only rice you can really use for paella. Stir it around for a bit, season with salt and pepper, add the ñora bits and some paprika. Moro suggest one teaspoon of sweet, smoked paprika. If you want to use some hot paprika too, go ahead. Then add enough hot chicken stock or water to just cover the rice. You can add more if it evaporates over the next fifteen minutes.

Then you're done. You can add the prawns or squid or whatever else you want at this stage.

On an August evening that felt like November, we ate old-fashioned carbonara and Pernilla complained of getting fat.

'But I want you to get fat. You should be getting fat,' I said. 'That's the point.'

The next hCG level was 67. It had nearly tripled in two days.

This was very good.

At Borough Market I had bought a duck, the fattiest of birds and not one I had ever cooked. I roasted it, making an intense gravy out of giblet stock, chopped cherries and lemon zest. I bought ricotta for my first gnocchi. On a hot evening we took plastic bags and bowls to a nearby railway station and stood on the platform picking blackberries while the commuters smiled.

'Come down here,' Pernilla said, 'these ones are massive.'

We walked off the platform and down the track a few yards, leaning into the thorny mass of plump, juicy berries. A train pulled in and the driver blared his horn at us, refusing to leave the station until we realized that it was us he was honking at. We sheepishly skipped back up to the platform with our plastic bags dripping purple and the train began to move.

'We're out of here,' Pernilla said. 'I'm not doing time for a bag of berries.'

At home I made blackberry ice, blackberry and rhubarb crumble, and I bought prosecco and made blackberry Bellinis for myself while I cooked. (Crush some blackberries through a sieve and fill a champagne glass about half full with the purée. Pour prosecco on top of it.)

The hCG level: 199. Again, it had nearly tripled in two further days. I asked the nurse if this meant the embryo was catching up to normal levels. It wasn't that simple, she said. It had started slowly, so only time and scans would tell.

It was a day between blood tests, and London's skies were the colour of the city's slate roofs. I stood at the sink, scrubbing clean the last of my vegetable patch's potatoes. The embryo's rate of growth, while still worrying, was something about which I had unfettered hope. And yet I was gloomy, without good cause, and the feeling was familiar.

I am eleven years old and it is Boxing Day in Edinburgh. I have just brushed my teeth in our upstairs bathroom, all red and black in a colour scheme done by the previous owners.

'Mum, I feel fed up,' I say to my mother, who has come in.

'What's wrong?' she says, knowing full well that this is just the come-down from the previous day's frenzy of gifts and feasting and expectation.

'I don't know,' I say. I lean against her; she puts her arms around me and I can smell her Chanel No. 5 and her cigarettes. Her long black hair gets in my face, tickling me. 'I can't think of anything in particular. I just feel fed up.'

I begin to cry. For no reason.

'It's OK to be fed up sometimes,' she says.

I stood looking out at the garden and dropped each potato – embarrassingly small, every one of them – into a colander. I turned round and picked up *French Provincial Cooking* to look at ways to do carrots and found 'Beurre Maître d'Hôtel', which began: 'We all know how to make parsley butter. But do we always do it really well or know its many uses?'

Elizabeth David made me laugh out loud, as she so often does. I heard my mother's voice often in the slightly patronizing, supremely confident, didactical sentences of her own cooking teacher. Once, when speaking to my father on the telephone, I read to him the three-sentence recipe for 'Les Oeufs en Cocotte à la Crème'. After the third and last sentence – 'This is one of the most delicious egg dishes ever invented, but it is rare to get it properly done' – my dad roared with the laughter of recognition.

'That's typical,' he said. He had thought that I was reading from my mother's own recipe book.

I followed Elizabeth David's strict instructions to chop the parsley very fine, my knife rocking backwards and forwards on the chopping board.

'Matty, could you get me some parsley, please?' I hear my mother say. I lift up the huge Georgian window frame overlooking the garden in Oxford Terrace, and there's the black window box full of curly parsley, whose very name makes my mouth water. I snip some sprigs and take it to her. And she chops it rapidly, automatically, with her Sabatier knife. I'm allowed to pinch some in my fingers, and its freshness fills my mouth.

The next day one of the Australian nurses called. 'Hi, Pernilla, it's Ashley from the clinic calling. Guess what your level is? It's up to 457,' she said. More than doubled in two days. On track.

'We're very happy with the levels.'

This was a serious change in tone from an organization that had clearly trained itself not to get its patients' hopes up. We began to mull over baby names. I wanted a girl – in my years of visiting war zones, I had not seen many women slaughtering children or anyone else for that matter – but I told Pernilla that I sensed it was a boy. We thought we would give a girl the middle name of Ann and a boy the middle name Jeffrey, after Pernilla's father.

And then something changed. Pernilla's body started to show signs that something might be wrong. Her hCG level climbed to 927, but the messages her body was giving out were bad. We went for gentle walks in almost total silence, not wanting to voice panic.

'Come in for your first scan on Tuesday,' the doctor told us that Saturday.

Over the weekend I walked around alone through the packed streets of west London during the Notting Hill Carnival, with a beer in my hand, the evening sun bronzing the dancing crowds. It was too hectic a scene for a woman trying to nurture a very new embryo. 'I'd love to take my kid to this one year,' I thought, as dads carried their little girls and boys on their shoulders through the kindly, spaced-out throng, kid headphones protecting their tender eardrums from the massive reggae beats that shook your whole body. I danced to blissed-out house music in a shoulder-to-shoulder crowd, then made my way home.

On the morning of the scan I wanted to be sick. Pernilla's symptoms of wrongness had worsened, and on the phone the doctor had mentioned the words 'ectopic' and 'non-viable'. Usually I did not go behind the screen for the scans, remaining in my seat across from the doctor's desk. On this occasion, I waited there while Pernilla undressed, staring at the fleur-de-lis pattern on the navy-blue screen and thinking of a similar material I had once bought at a street market in Cairo. And then, because this was such a crucial examination, I asked her if I could come and stand next to her and take a look at what the doctor was seeing on the ultrasound.

'Of course,' she said.

I joined her behind the screen and stared at the ultrasound monitor as the doctor moved the wand. It was grey and black and fibrous in there, I could see that much. But otherwise I didn't know what I was looking at – or for. I had a vague sense that what I wanted was for the doctor to point out a small bean-shaped thing with a slight heartbeat.

'To be honest, Pernilla,' he said, 'I can't see anything.'

'Look harder; look again,' I wanted to scream. 'You can't see anything clearly on the screen, so you just need to look again.'

Those hCG readings were coming from somewhere.

'It could be ectopic,' he said, and my Internet research was enough so that I knew an ectopic pregnancy – where the embryo had attached itself to somewhere other than the wall of the uterus – would mean no baby and a threat to Pernilla's health.

When we got back home from the clinic, there were some pieces of junk mail on the floor, stuffed through the letterbox in spite of the 'No Junk Mail' sticker I had attached to it. Some of them, I admit, had been there for a few days. But they sent me into a sudden rage. On top of the small pile of shiny, colourful pieces of paper was an ad for a pizza-delivery place. It was one of several from the same pizzeria that had landed on the doormat. I dialled the phone number that was printed in red numerals along the top and bottom of the flier.

'Pizza delivery.'

'Is that the manager?' I asked, literally shaking with fury.

'Yes, sir. Can I help?'

'I have a "No Junk Mail" sticker clearly attached to my door,' I said. 'Why have you just stuffed a handful of fliers through my letterbox? Have you ever heard of global warming or recyling?'

The man tried to say something.

'No, no, listen to me – I'm going to sue you,' I said, my voice rising. 'You're breaking the law.' I had no idea if that was true. 'And I'll be reporting you to the council.'

I put down the phone and called a lighting shop, whose flier happened to be next up in the small pile that lay in front of me on the table. I repeated my furious, indignant protest at their wanton destruction of the planet for monetary gain, and made the same meaningless legal threats.

'OK, I'll give the manager your message,' the woman in the lighting shop said. Her tone indicated that she might not deliver the message in the most sympathetic way. Her tone indicated: get a life, you twat.

'Did you just call one of those delivery places?' Pernilla asked me from the kitchen, where she was making a cup of tea. She seemed mildly amused, but not very.

I didn't phone any other offenders. It was not making me feel any better, getting angry at strangers. I felt guilty, shitty. I put their fliers in the recycling. We waited.

The doctor called later in the day. Pernilla, already lying on our bed, answered. I came into the room when I heard the phone ring. Pernilla picked it up.

'Three hundred,' she said, obviously repeating what she'd just been told. Her voice was steady but entirely flat. 'Oh, OK, thanks. Bye.'

The hCG level was just over 300. It should have been around 3,000. I sat on the floor next to the bed and held her arm as she cried. Then my body began to heave.

A few days later, the clinic assured us that the pregnancy hadn't been ectopic. We felt a brief blip of relief but it soon faded into sadness. A week later – a week of doing nothing and making excuses to editors – I went out with friends for lunch and drank until it was very late.

*　*　*

'Why do you drink so much whisky?' I ask my mother. We're in her bedroom. She's in bed. It's the early evening of an early-summer day. I am sixteen years old, and I keep hoping that alcohol will return to being something that makes my mother happy, not unconscious.

'I just feel so sad sometimes, Matthew,' she says. 'It makes the sadness go away.'

26

Remembering, or prompting memory, requires effort. I had made the decision to remember, to conjure my good mother up from the past to allow her to take her rightful place alongside the terrible mother who loomed so unavoidably in my memories. I had deliberately set – even contrived – the conditions for this kitchen séance: cooking, reading her cookery books and others of my own, exploring her past through conversations with her siblings and my sister and my father. Then I had to sit back and see what happened. And with the help of these stimuli, with my memory pores open, the glimpses of my good mother had come at unexpected moments, leaping in front of my eyes, fully formed but ethereal, needing to be put down on paper before they drifted away again.

But there was a limit to how far I seemed to want to go. I sat for weeks and then months ignoring her own recipe book, except for the one time when I'd opened it looking for the strawberry ice cream recipe. I left family photographs unseen in their albums, home movies unplayed on DVDs, the boxes with her papers inside unopened. I made no efforts to get her medical records, to speak to her doctors, to track down key biographical details – all the kinds of basic reporting I knew how to do with my eyes closed.

On the second morning after the doctor called Pernilla to tell us the pregnancy was over, I went back to the Farm Street church on my own and sat in the chapel of Our Lady of Lourdes, the miracle mother. I had planned to not get angry, to not ask for anything, but to thank my mother and God's mother for their efforts, ghost prayers from an unbeliever. But that was bullshit. It was dishonest. I was angry. And I wanted something. I was there to make an appeal, not to be meek.

'Look, I'm not going to lie. I want a baby, OK?' I said to myself silently in the chapel. Another man, about my age, sat two yards away, unable to suppress his sobs at his own private tragedy. I wanted to put my hand on his shoulder and go to a bar with him so that we could share our problems and part later in a fraternity of hope. I looked up at the marble statue of the Virgin.

'You had a kid,' I said to the graceful sculpture. 'Mum, you had two. You have to help Pernilla. She just wants to be a mother too. Come on.'

I sat around the house for two more weeks, pretending to editors and my wife and myself that I was working hard in my study.

Then one day I picked up two stained silver napkin rings that had sat on a shelf in my study since my sister and I had found them in a box after our mother died. One was inscribed, on the inside, with: 'Matthew 2.11.69'. The other was older, and on the outside were the initials JRRT. Inside, the date: '2nd Sept. 1950'. John Taylor, my mother's little brother, who died of meningitis after six or seven weeks. They were christening rings, mine and my dead infant uncle's. Somehow these mementoes of birth and, in John's case, early death, sparked me back into action. It was time to start being a reporter again, to look at my mother's papers, her recipes, the home movies, to make some calls and piece things together. I would have to accept that some of what I would find would be painful.

27

Sandwiched between three major roads in north-west London is an island that is home to a pub, some shops and the Odeon Swiss Cottage cinema. It is an early February evening in 1943. German bombs continue to fall, ripping chunks out of London's architecture, but in these cold winter days there is some good news on the Pathé newsreel: the Germans have just surrendered in Stalingrad, a crushing defeat for Hitler and a turning point in the war that has been grinding on for nearly four years. Christian Taylor has left her only child, Jennifer, with a babysitter and is enjoying a night out with her husband, Bobby. She is gazing up at the screen when an intense ache pops up in her back and moves quickly to the front of her body. It lasts for a surprisingly long time and then the cramp fades. But it's back again soon. My grandmother has been through this before. She's about to give birth.

'The baby's coming,' my grandmother whispers in Bobby's ear – or so goes the story that is years later passed down to my aunt Jennifer and, later still, to me.

My grandfather is a passionate patriot. He worships Churchill, detests Hitler and wants to be up to date on the progress of the war. 'I'm not taking you out now,' he says firmly. 'I'm watching the news.'

They slip out of the Odeon after the newsreel has finished.

Jennifer Taylor is two years and ten months old when she first sets her eyes on my mother, Ann Pauline Taylor, her new baby sister. Christian and Bobby Taylor are comfortably off, but their moderate affluence has not prevented their nanny from being called up for national service. So when Christian is about to give birth, she puts her daughter Jennifer into a children's home for two weeks. The day of the meeting of the sisters, Bobby picks up Jennifer from her hated children's home in a black taxi and takes her into the kitchen on the ground floor of the three-bedroom flat in the red-brick, semi-detached house to see the new baby. Ann is in a Moses basket on the kitchen worktop. Christian hands Jennifer a glass of milk and lifts her up so she can take her first look at her new sister. The baby has a tiny birthmark under her nostril on the right side of her face.

Christian pushes the small navy-blue pram up the street they live on towards the nearby department store. They pass the little convent school at the end of their street, which Jennifer attends, walking to and from it with a Catholic neighbour who also goes to the school. At the rear of the department store is a door where people queue up for their wartime rations – some milk, a few eggs. My grandmother and my aunt, with my mother buried under blankets in the pram, join the queue.

Sometimes, when the bombing of London is particularly heavy, Christian sends Jennifer and Ann north on the train to Edinburgh. They stay in a basement room in the Scotia Hotel, which is owned by my great-grandmother, Christian's mother, an Irishwoman named Marian McLaughlin. They call her Gaga, because they cannot pronounce Grandmother or Granny. Gaga drinks a lot and, for all her success in running the hotel in Edinburgh's smart New Town, as a member of Edinburgh's marginalized Catholic community she is generally not welcome in Protestant circles. The family's friends are nearly all Catholics.

When they move back to Edinburgh after the war, Bobby Taylor begins to film his growing family on a cine camera. Amid the fur coats and the cigarettes and ties – rarely is an adult man seen in these home movies without a tie – my mother appears.

A baby at first, she slowly grows into a grinning, pretty little girl with a gap in her upper front teeth. She often wears a ribbon in her black hair and always, in every shot, shrugs a little in her shy excitement about being filmed. There are white ankle socks and dresses and skirts, never trousers. She squirms when an adult tries to hold her hand. She edges slowly into the cold North Sea on the beach at North Berwick, along the coast from Edinburgh. She grows older, and the three sisters – Jennifer, Ann and little Kata – dance around in the garden, with my mother holding one hand behind her back, displaying the dance moves she has been studying. She leaps with her sisters and friends through a sprinkler on the lawn. At five or six, with bows in her hair, she dances on the patio of the house at Blackbarony Road, performing pas de deux and lifting the hems of the kilt she is wearing. It is the day of her First Communion, and she stands in the garden dressed like a child bride, flowers and a white lace veil draped from her crown, a white cape over her shoulders, her hands together in prayer. She is a little older, perhaps seven, and again she dances in the back garden, in a ballerina's light-blue tutu, pirouetting among the daisies on her pointed toe, curtsying formally when her routine is finished.

My grandmother, it seems, was not entirely keen on children. In the home movies she is charismatic and stylish but not visibly affectionate to her daughters. During several summer vacations, Jennifer, my mother, and Kata are sent off to stay with cousins in Ireland. The ferry takes them from Glasgow to Derry. They spend happy, if motherless, weeks running around barefoot, with no running water, no electricity, paraffin lamps in the evenings, peat burning in the fireplace, three to a bed. One summer, my mother catches pneumonia, and my grandmother flies to Ireland to fetch her and her sisters home.

Jennifer is in charge of her sisters for much of the time, taking them to the Catholic day school, St Margaret's, on Edinburgh's trams, or to the zoo or the skating rinks or riding stables. The nanny accompanies them at times. They play hide-and-seek and other games in the woods near their house on Blackford Hill and in the quarry nearby. They know when to be home for meals.

My mother is showing signs of being a very bright girl, but there is nothing she loves more than ballet. She is a natural and takes endless classes until, one day, she auditions for the Royal Ballet School. This London institution is the best in Britain, the home of many of Britain's finest dancers. To gain a place at the Royal Ballet School is to be given a chance at making dancing your life.

My mother is accepted at the age of ten. Her father decides his daughter is too young to go to boarding school in London. She is deeply disappointed and becomes, for a time, quiet and passive. She and Jennifer and later Kata become boarders at the Kilgraston Convent School in Perthshire, a strict place where the nuns use hand-held clickers to silence the girls, to make them sit down, to make them stand up. My mother sits for a nationwide exam at the age of eleven and she achieves the highest score in Scotland. At prize-giving each year, she picks up piles of books. She graduates at sixteen and has to fill a year before she's old enough to go to university. So her parents send her and Jennifer to a Catholic, French-speaking finishing school in a convent at the top of the Spanish Steps in Rome.

'There was duchess so and so, princess so and so, with her daughter so and so,' Jennifer recalls. 'Some of them were absolutely charming. We met a very nice German girl whose father, von Stauffenberg, had been executed by Hitler during the war. He was the German who tried to ... you know, von Stauffenberg. Well, his daughter was there, the duchess. They were very well connected because her aunt was married to the papal ambassador to Rome at that time, so we would go to the papal ambassador and his wife's house for swimming.'

The sisters, with a good friend from Edinburgh, yawn their

way through lectures in churches and museums and run around the magical city in the afternoon. It is 1960, and *La Dolce Vita* is on in the cinemas, so they sit in the darkness watching the impossibly handsome Marcello Mastroianni seduce his way around the city.

They crane their necks at the Sistine Chapel and work on their tans on the beaches during days off. They go to the opera and a party at the British embassy to celebrate the Queen's birthday. The nuns take them on a long bus tour of Naples, Capri, Assisi, Siena, Florence, Pompeii and Pisa. They learn absolutely nothing practical or useful in the four months in which they are being polished into young ladies. It is all gelato and Italian boys and beauty.

After finishing school is finished, Jennifer, Ann and their friend Susie go to Venice and Bologna on their own. And then the sisters take the train to Antibes, to meet the rest of the family to water-ski and sit on the beach.

My mother doesn't know it but these independent travels around Europe echo trips her future mentor Elizabeth David made as a young woman many years earlier, going to a finishing school in Germany and living with a family in Paris while she studied at the Sorbonne, exploring the canals and rivers of France on a journey she took in 1939, aged twenty-five, with war about to break out in Europe. Elizabeth David's first experience of Italy was when she and her Jewish lover, Charles Gibson Cowan, were arrested by the Italian Fascists, who had that day declared war on Britain, allying themselves with Nazi Germany. Blessedly, especially for Cowan, they were released and allowed to sail on through the Mediterranean to Greece. Years later, by then a famous food writer, Elizabeth David visited many of the same places my mother was to visit, discovering a national cuisine barely known or respected in Britain. Her *Italian Food* helped give birth to a British love affair with Parmesan, mozzarella and Parma ham that has never waned.

162

My mother has the idea of going to Oxford to study medicine, but her father, wanting to keep his daughters in their home town, says no. She accepts a place at Edinburgh University and fills some more of the months before university with a second finishing school, in Garmisch-Partenkirchen.

Or that was the story I heard, anyway. 'I wanted to be a doctor, but your grandfather wouldn't let me,' my mother told me several times over the years.

I am not sure now how true that is. As her illness worsened, my mother tended to blame other people for her disappointments.

Royal Botanic Garden in Edinburgh

28

Not every recipe I learned and wrote into my recipe book had to be edible. Sometimes it seemed appropriate to try something liquid. I made up this drink – although I realized later that quite a few people beat me to it – just before looking for the first time at my mother's papers. I took the glass with me to the spare room, where the two box files and one suitcase had sat under a side table for months.

❧

Persian Cosmopolitan

You can vary the amounts below, depending on how stiff the task ahead, but I suggest you keep the same proportions.

One ounce of vodka.

Half an ounce of pomegranate juice. If you can juice your own, all the better.

Half an ounce of triple sec or Cointreau. Fresh pomegranate juice is pretty bitter, more so than a Cosmopolitan's usual cranberry, so be ready to up the triple sec or Cointreau according to taste.

Half an ounce of fresh lime juice.

Shake all that up in a cocktail shaker or, if you don't have one, in a tall glass with some ice.

At the same time, rub a slice of lime around the rim of a

martini glass. Sprinkle some sugar on to a side plate. Tip the martini glass upside down and press it into the sugar, creating a light rim of sugar (too much is just sickly). To spice it up even more, you can mix some ground cardamom and nutmeg into the sugar. Again, not too much.

Pour the booze into the glass. If you want, you can add a lime twist or a few pomegranate seeds.

When I laid the faux-snakeskin, musty-smelling suitcase that held some of my mother's papers flat on the carpet, I guessed I would not be opening up a trove of happy mementoes. That's why it had taken me so long to look inside, I suspected. For most of my life I had kept my own memories of those years carefully packed away in some part of my brain. I knew they were there, didn't like what was in them, rarely discussed the detailed contents with friends from my early days or with family – because we all knew, we all had our own versions, we didn't ever need reminding, we wanted to forget – and when someone I had not met before asked me about my parents, I would usually end that line of enquiry with a quick answer. 'My dad's a sculptor, and my mother's very mentally ill,' I would say, as if it were her chosen career, and the work colleague or the blind date and I would silently agree to move the conversation on.

I pushed the two latches on the suitcase lock to the side and opened it up.

On top of the pile of files, envelopes, rolled-up diplomas and albums was a brown A4-size envelope from Penguin Books. And another from Oxford University Press. They immediately caught my eye, and since these folders and envelopes and albums did not seem to be in any order, I just started there.

Inside were standard rejection letters, dated 1996. 'Dear Ann McAllester, Thank you for your letter regarding your poetry ...' And, attached by a paper clip, dozens of pages of photocopied poems in my mother's handwriting. I skimmed through many of them. They were not good, but they let me into my mother's mind. One long poem, dated 21 May 1996, was entitled 'Death', and it ends:

> I will go into
> The earth
> One day
> And decay,
> Until only my bones
> Shall show.
> Where will I be then?
> Matthew
> Won't be able
> Then
> To phone me.
> My grandchildren
> Won't be able, then,
> To sit on my knee,
> And play with my hair
> Because I will be dead,
> Then.
> But what of my presence [*sic*] state
> Then?
> What will it be?
> What is it now?
> For I live in a dream.

Deeper into the packed suitcase were more poems, hundreds of them, manically scribbled during the years I had spent in New York, the place to which I fled as soon as I was able. The poems reminded me of the evening courses she took in Edinburgh when I was about ten. She'd spent hours poring over Seamus Heaney, Ted Hughes, Sylvia Plath (not, perhaps, the right reading for my mother), and rereading *Ulysses*, over and over again. Then came her own poetry. None of it was much good but parts were somewhat revealing:

The Fifth Decade

1943 Infant, female, born in London. Parents.
1953 Skinny wee lass, lank-legged.
1963 Bride
1973 Beautiful, arrogant, mother
1983 Stripped, pared to her only self; herself pared to a
staggering cowering creature in a psychiatric hospital
The fifth decade ... Shelley Season of mists

The poetry reached its prodigious, awful zenith in the mid-1990s, as the bulging contents of the suitcase made only too clear. I did not read it all.

There were also notebooks filled with detailed writings on the Bible, Nietzsche, *Tristan and Isolde*, Wittgenstein, Auschwitz, Babylon, Hiroshima, the Hapsburgs, Martin Luther King, Greek plays, Gnosticism, Camus, and on and on. There was a notebook of Greek vocabulary, from the time she'd decided, when I was a teenager, to study for a degree in theology in Edinburgh. Among the notes, the names and addresses of two priests she became obsessed with and stalked. I found a folder that contained the legal correspondence surrounding her divorce from my father, which I glanced at briefly until I decided that it was, fundamentally, none of my business. I unsealed two more large envelopes of poems, never looked at since she'd sealed them years ago.

Another notebook had my old address in Brooklyn scribbled on the inside cover, opposite a diagram that featured the word 'Auschwitz' in the centre and seemed to depict some relationship between Persians, Britannicus (from Racine?), Sleeping Beauty, Nero, and Tzonis (which I looked up on the Internet – a professor of architecture, including classical architecture, seemed to be the only possible connection. It was, possibly, a made-up name). In the pages that followed there were notes on her reading: Foucault (rubbish!), Sartre, Nietzsche again. In a cardboard tube were diplomas: a BA from Edinburgh University; typing and copying diplomas from a secretarial college in London; teaching diplomas enabling her to teach in primary and secondary schools. I found a file on her intermittent years of teaching in Edinburgh, a half-hearted career that came and went over the course of twenty years, and the first thing I pulled out was a letter, never opened, offering her a temporary job in the autumn of 1986 (she taught French and history). 'But she was completely mad in 1986,' I thought. Crazy but often functional, always intimidating and well spoken, and articulate to the point of pedantic even when she was drunk or delusional. She was a madwoman with wonderful syntax. That same year, another head teacher thought better of offering her work. Writing from his school near Edinburgh, this head teacher commends my mother's teaching skills and personality but suggests she isn't quite up to teaching special education.

The files seemed to show that 1986 marked the end of her teaching.

I found some pieces of unlined A4 paper, typed and titled 'Diary'. My guess is that it was written around 1993.

'1 July. Spoke to no one except shop people in Waterstones and Thins [an Edinburgh bookshop],' she writes.

On 3 July she seems to describe a dream:

My grandmother has come back as a magician (she is dead). She's absolutely lovely, as in life, and I adore her. There's nothing I can do for her because she's in heaven so she's happy. She asked me what she could do for me and I told her I wanted to be transported back to Port an Droighionn with d1 [whom I take to mean my father, Don] and the children when they were little. That is impossible so I've asked her to arrange that in ten years' time I shall often be at Port an Droig.

with my children and their children and d1. She has told me that that will be difficult but that she will try. I gave her a big kiss and a hug.

4 July. Have seen no one today ... Today is Sunday, which I hate. Haven't spoken to anyone ... Wrote to the children. I yearn for them in my pain. I need them with me now and I can't have them because they are far away and busy and happy. It's a beautiful day. I wanted to go to the beach.

5 July. So depressed in morning had to force myself to go out.

I randomly chose another letter. It was open and was dated 17 December 1986. It was from the headmaster of the Catholic boarding school in Lancashire that my grandfather and uncle attended. 'I am sorry', the headmaster writes, 'that you are having trouble with your son Matthew but ... I am unable to help since all our sixth form places are filled this year.'

There was another letter testifying to her attempts to ship me off, from another leading Catholic boarding school's head-master, who explained to my mother that he did not like to accept boys who did not want to attend his school.

'Can I have this back please when you have read it – M. knows about it!' my mother had written in red ink, presumably to my father, from whom she had been divorced for three years by that time. And then I remembered: I had seen this letter before. It was a year of war between my mother and me.

One afternoon I find a letter lying on the kitchen table, opened, its return address clear: Ampleforth College, York. I know the letter must be about me. I read it. And when my mother comes home, I am not respectful.

'Fuck you,' I yell at her. 'You need to understand. I am never going to any fucking boarding school. I hate living here, but there is no fucking way I am ever going to boarding school.'

I go to my bedroom and punch the door, slightly dislodging one of the panels from the frame. I begin to mount a campaign to live on my own, in a studio flat, reasoning with my parents that, seeing as they have ruined my life, the very least they can do for me is to let me live on my own, away from them. This is an unsuccessful campaign.

Most teachers I have at secondary school take me aside at some point over the years to tell me that my mother has been in touch and that 'I understand things are difficult at home'. One of them explains to me that school rules would not allow me to live alone, even if my parents green-lighted and funded my escape fantasy to my own flat.

My end-of-term reports make regular, implicit references to something going wrong at home: 'When he has sorted out his present unhappiness he is going to really enjoy life,' my teacher writes, when I am twelve.

'I am so pleased he has settled again,' the same teacher writes when I am thirteen. 'It was not nice to see him so sad.'

'Matthew has been more settled this term,' writes another when I am fifteen.

'Matthew prefers to be self-contained, which requires him to give off signals that all is well and under control,' the same teacher writes, later in the same year.

Away from the chaos of home, I look to girls for comfort. And I take it all a little too seriously, having my heart crushed at the age of fifteen, running away to the Highlands on a train, and sleeping in a field in the rain for a night. That defeats me and I return home – to a telling-off from two unimpressed policemen. Teenage girls, I realize when it's far too late, can't offer me an alternative to a happy family.

But they do offer real joys. In 1987, when I am seventeen, I meet a beautiful blonde girl named Clara. She's going through a brief Goth phase when we meet. She plays the violin and gets caught shoplifting jewellery. We go out to pubs in the dark streets of Edinburgh and get drunk among friends. For the first time in my life I am regularly having sex – in Edinburgh's private gardens at night (scaling spiked railings, spreading my jacket out on the sloping grass for Clara like a teenage Walter Raleigh draping his cape over the puddle for his queen), at a bus stop, in spare rooms of houses where we are babysitting. Before Clara, it had been snatched moments. This is different and amazing. We have friends – two sisters – with a big house and parents so alcoholic and dysfunctional that every weekend their house fills up with teenagers drinking cheap wine, making coq au vin, flirting on the sofa in front of Mickey Rourke movies, making love in the bedrooms upstairs. Often, I don't call home to say where I am. I know my mother is sedated by Scotch and pills and, besides, fuck her. Why should I call? At other times I stash Clara in my bedroom. My friend Stefano also has a beautiful girlfriend. The four of us writhe under quilts on the two beds in my room one Friday evening as my mother cooks dinner downstairs. We're unashamed by our proximity, but also too young to be turned on by it, merely seizing the rare opportunity to have sex in a comfortable bed. My mother leaves us alone, not imagining that an orgy is going on above her head. We giggle as the twenty minutes of the same record – by the Communards – come to an end once again; I get up from on top of Clara, put the stylus back on the vinyl and 'Don't Leave Me This Way' begins for the sixth time. The door is locked, and when my mother calls up the stairs we troop down, flushed, for a meal, with laughing looks, and we return for more Communards afterwards.

On a Saturday night while my mother, upstairs, lies under the heavy quilt of her sleeping pills, Clara and I hold each other in my narrow single bed. In the morning Clara sneaks out the front door while my mother is in the rear of the house. A few days later Clara's mother calls to thank mine for allowing Clara to stay the night. I have no defence for my deception and don't bother to mount one. My mother has long since forsaken her right to impose rules, I have decided.

173

'Your mother tells me you had Clara over to stay and lied about it,' my father says on the phone, from his small house in a mews on the other side of town. My sister and I spend one night a week there. 'She also tells me you don't mind your Ps and Qs.'

He is more enquiring than angry, and I think I sense an amused admiration for my sneaking a girl in under Mum's nose and a sympathy for what drives me to use bad language towards my mother. Perhaps there's some guilt in there, perhaps some yearning to make things better somehow.

'Yeah,' I say, 'that's true.' I do not apologize.

I'm angry that he's managed to get out of a situation that he helped to create, one that I'm stuck with, one that was not of my making.

'It's not much fun living here,' I say. I know he knows that already. His house has a small spare room, but I don't want to move there. My mother is the victim here, I believe, and for all her raging and drinking I feel loyal to her. My sister has left home for college, and my mother would be left alone for the first time in her life. Besides, I live this kind of unfettered life without rules that I know would end if I moved in with him. I tell him again that I want to get out of here but I don't want to live with him either. So I stay. And the war intensifies.

Later that year, I am with my mother in the car, driving out of the psychiatric hospital. My mother now has regular appointments there, and I go along sometimes while she sees her doctor. I sit in the car or amble around the grounds.

'The doctor thinks you should see someone here in the Young People's Unit,' my mother says as we drive home, referring to the part of the hospital that is for children and young adults with severe psychiatric problems. She and I have been arguing a lot. On a recent evening I had picked up her small tape player and thrown it across the kitchen, smashing it.

'Excuse me? You're the crazy one. I don't have a problem.'

*   *   *

174

When I thought about the hospital, for the first time in a long while, I began to wonder about her illness, to ask myself a question I had years ago given up asking: could the doctors have treated her more effectively? Could they have fixed her? As I went through her papers, I remembered my fury at the doctors who could not or would not see that she was desperately mad and needed help. As far as I knew at the time, they diagnosed her as depressed and an alcoholic. When she went back to the hospital in Edinburgh, it was to the Alcohol Problems Unit. But the alcohol was just a symptom of her madness. How could psychiatrists not see this but a teenage boy could? My sister felt the same way.

'They treated her like a drunk,' she told me, when I asked her if she, too, felt the doctors had let our mother down.

Did it need to happen, the lost twenty-five years of my mother's life? Was it unavoidable, my making do without a mother for most of my life? If she had been diagnosed and treated earlier, would she have been able to control her alcoholism? Would her body not have been so brutalized and bashed around until it gave up? Would she have lived a happy life? Would she still be here with me? Would I not be someone who had hidden with great comfort in the fury of other people's wars but who now walked through the streets of London feeling unprotected, afflicted at times with a vague sense of fear because my mother could now never defend me, could never dive into the sea to save me from drowning?

Perhaps it would do me no good to see the documentation of mistakes. My father wondered aloud if this was such a good idea.

'These are deep and dangerous waters that you are going into,' my uncle Paul, my mother's brother, warned me.

Pernilla worried too but she was patient and quietly let me do what I needed to.

I had to work it out. After all, I'm a reporter. It's my instinct to ask, to dig, to uncover. I usually work best if I'm angry, if someone in a position of power has done something bad to someone who is helpless, and I had begun to feel the traces of an anger inside me whose size and power scared me. I suppose I had felt it many years ago, but I had sat on it and forgotten it. The life my mother should have had. The mother I should have had.

It was a bit silly, but I decided to look up which famous, successful people had been born in the same month and year my mother had been born. People whose lives had worked out. Joe Pesci. David Geffen. The economist Joseph Stiglitz. Mike Leigh and Michael Mann, film directors. George Harrison. Howell Raines, a famous editor of the *New York Times* (one day older than my mother). Blythe Danner, the actress – and mother of Gwyneth Paltrow – who is as beautiful now as my mother could have been (three days older than my mother).

Had someone made a catastrophic mistake? Had someone in a hospital had it within their power to keep my mother sane and happy, to let her have a full life?

I don't believe in suing doctors. They do their best and their best is usually miraculous and beautiful, acts of life and love. We all make mistakes. I just wanted to know if someone had made a mistake with my mother.

I asked a friend who works in the healthcare world if I had a legal right to my mother's medical records. I did, he believed.

I called the local government office in my part of London that stores medical records. In the NHS, a patient's medical records are meant to follow him or her around for life, from doctor's surgery to doctor's surgery, from birth to death.

'My mother died a while ago, and I'm trying to get hold of her medical records,' I said to the lady who answered the phone when I called the local healthcare trust.

'Why do you want them? Are you working with a lawyer?' she asked.

'No, I'm not. I just want to see them for personal reasons,' I said. 'I don't have a lawyer.'

The lady said I had to make a written request and they'd send me copies. Perhaps. There would be a charge of ten pounds and I'd have to pay for the photocopies. I said I was fine with that.

29

While I waited for the medical records, I continued to report on my mother's life. The process, the sensation of discovery in and of itself came to give me a pleasure and comfort I had never got on any other story.

Once I knew my mother had been born in London and christened close to where I now lived, I wanted to find her first address. I wanted to look at the house to which she had been taken when her parents brought her home as a newborn baby. I could not find her birth certificate among her papers, and her siblings could not remember the address, even though my aunt Jennifer could visualize the house. My uncle Paul, the youngest of the four siblings, thought his parents had lived in Harrow-on-the-Hill during the war, in suburban north London.

There was a clue in something Jennifer, the oldest, remembered: the name of the department store at the end of the road where they would collect their rations during the war was John Barnes, she told me on the phone from Rhode Island. An Internet search indicated that John Barnes had been located on Finchley Road, in West Hampstead. There was a supermarket in a lovely old modernist building on Finchley Road. I called it and the automated answering message said: 'Welcome to Waitrose John Barnes.' Now I knew my grandparents must have lived in West Hampstead, not Harrow-on-the-Hill. It was very close to where I now lived. But which street? Which house?

I called the church where my mother had been christened

and where we had held her funeral and asked if they had a record of the christening. The lady who took my first call did not get back to me. An Irish lady took the second call and within an hour called me back, saying she was putting a copy of the certificate in the post for me.

'Does it have the address on it?' I asked.

'Oh, I didn't look. Let me see,' she said. 'Forty-five Compayne Gardens.'

Of all the streets in London. Almost twenty years ago, I had stayed in a flat in Compayne Gardens. The father of my college girlfriend, Sophie, lived there at that point. Until I moved back to London after covering the war in Iraq, it remained one of only a handful of places that were familiar to me in the city of my birth. I dug out an old address book. Sophie's father had lived at 43 Compayne Gardens. I had stayed several times in the house next to my mother's first home. London is a big city.

My uncle Paul remembered his father talking about how the Jewish family next door, émigrés from pre-war Europe, had had the foresight to have a rather smart bomb shelter built in their garden. My grandparents, carrying Jennifer – aged three or four – and my infant mother, would climb over the garden wall to the neighbours' house during German bombing raids and shelter with the Jewish family in their state-of-the-art concrete bunker.

My own memory rushed back to the front of Sophie's father's building: the blue plaque noting that a famous Zionist had lived there once. I drove the short distance to Compayne Gardens. There was 45, my mother's first home. And there on number 43 was the blue plaque, which noted that Nahum Sokolow had lived in that house until 1936, the year of his death. I remembered a street in Tel Aviv named Sokolow. And a quick bit of research told me he had been a Russian/Polish journalist and Zionist leader who had translated into Hebrew for the first time the great Zionist leader Theodor Herzl's utopian novel *Altneuland*. Was it the Sokolow family

– perhaps his widow or children – who had sheltered my infant mother from Nazi bombs in my ex-girlfriend's garden, which I had wandered around at the age of twenty?

Sophie spoke with her father. Yes, there had been a bomb shelter in the garden, long since removed when they lived there, but you could still see where it had been.

My mother's traces and mine kept crossing. There were other coincidences and connections: I sometimes shopped at the Waitrose John Barnes on Finchley Road. I often saw films at the Odeon Swiss Cottage, where I now know my mother first began to push her way into the world. When I met my wife, she was living a few minutes from the Odeon on a street in Swiss Cottage named Eton Avenue. When my sister found a nursing home for my mother, a good and caring and pretty place for her to live in peace, it was on Eton Avenue. You can walk from Eton Avenue to Compayne Gardens, from my mother's last home to her first, in about ten minutes, passing almost by the Odeon and directly past the Waitrose on the way.

Coincidence may just be the criss-crossing of time and place, worthless but for the brief raising of an eyebrow and the tingle of discovery. But for me, coincidence had come to provide a feeling of continuity and belonging and history. Until very recently, London had seemed a massive, amorphous sprawl to me, despite the fact that I had spent my first years here, because there had been such a long period during which I had exiled myself – from Britain, from my family, from my past, from my mother. But now the streets and houses and shops and cinemas of north-west London, a place I could not have found on the map four years earlier, seemed to vibrate with a sense of belonging. I felt like a salmon finding the river of my birth after a transatlantic swim, or a migratory water buffalo following ancestral routes through African plains. The Comanches, a friend told me, believed that a person's ghost would return to the place where the person had spent most of his or her life even if they had died in a distant land. I had been born here. My mother's first home was here. Her happiest days, as a young wife and mother in the 1960s and early 1970s, had been spent here. She had returned here for her final years, her last moments of happiness, as if to die in her true home.

And after years of living in foreign countries, of hiding in the lives and deaths of others, I, too, had come here, come to a place where all around me were strands of a web connecting me to my mother's happy, sane life.

I knew none of this when she was alive.

Sometimes I wanted to get down on my knees on the pavement to thank this corner of this huge city for tidying up a few things that had long seemed lost for ever.

Later, when going through my mother's papers again, I found this passage in a diary she wrote while in hospital:

I was born in London during the Blitz. My mother said that she went into labour in the Odeon, Swiss Cottage, and that my father wouldn't leave until after the news ... I remember being very upset once because there was a deluge on and my sister Jennifer was at nursery. I remember the rocking horse there, and my mother giving us ice cream at Peter Barnes [she must mean John Barnes]. I remember being in a cot at my grandmother's in Edinburgh and I remember us having a nanny in a uniform whom we both hated, and I remember being wheeled down Dublin Street in a pushchair and the bumpy feeling of the runnelled pavement. That's all I remember about the war.

Preparing crab at Port an Droighionn

30

I'd prefer that the following were not true. It spoils the picture somewhat. But it was also in my newly beloved corner of London where our family began to unravel more than thirty-five years ago.

The phone rings in my father's studio. 'Don,' my mother says, and my father hears a voice he has never heard before. 'The builders ...' She is sobbing. There's trouble with the Irish builders who are working in their new house in Little Venice: 15 Ashworth Road. Often there are clients in my father's studio – art directors, marketing people, magazine editors – and, depending on the product, there can also be a collection of cooks, artists, models, hand models with immense patience and perfectly formed hands and, always, my father's assistants. On this morning, in the early summer of 1971, they are preparing for a shoot, they're not in the middle of one, and so it's easy for my father to step into the sunshine and hail a black cab.

Within half an hour he is home, at the large detached house he has just bought, a few blocks to the north of Elizabeth Close. There are two children now. Our parents feel that my sister and I need a garden; my mother needs a larger kitchen; the au pair needs a room. And so a team of builders has been in the house for nearly two months, building my mother's dream kitchen, knocking down a wall, taking out fireplaces and replacing them with fashionable gas fires, rewiring, repainting, replacing bathrooms and flooring, painting inside and out. It has been going on a long time, and in recent days it has caused some tension. But my father thinks it's just the normal stuff that happens when there are people in your house, making a mess and invading your space.

The taxi pulls up outside the house on the broad, tree-lined street, and my father walks through the house. It's supposed to be full of painters and plumbers and plasterers. There is no one there. Just a lot of mess – hammers, paintbrushes, cans of paint. He walks through the hall to the kitchen and out the French doors into the garden. My mother is sitting on the grass at the bottom of the garden, her back to the house. She is crying, extremely upset. My father sits next to her on the lawn. He puts his arm around her and gently asks her what the matter is.

'One of the builders draped his jacket over the armchair that's in the pile of furniture next to the sitting-room door,' she says through her sobs.

'Yes,' my father says.

'And I threw it into the garden,' she says.

'The jacket?'

'Yes,' she says.

That's not the whole story, as my father finds out when, a bit later, he calls his friend who is working as the architect on the project. My mother accompanied the jacket-throwing with enough obscenities and fury to convince the squad of tough-skinned Irish builders that they'd had enough.

My parents sit in the garden for a long time, talking it through, my mother slowly calming down. My father has always known she can be fiery and he has long loved her for it. He grew up in a household of manners, order and temperance. She and two sisters and one brother and her parents are louder in normal talk, often, than most people are in argument. They argue and shout and adore one another. My mother is an unbearable, unapologetic snob, and when people don't meet her expectations, whether she is talking in a shop with a sluggish sales assistant or at a dinner where her fellow guests are debating architectural preservation, she is merciless. She is also the warmest of hosts, drawing people into her world with her frankness and quick wit and willingness to listen and give back. My father has spent years with her, and often they talk for hours and never once has he found a word she says to be boring. She is never dismissive of him.

He has never seen her like this before. She is overwhelmed, angry, frustrated, unable to cope. Because of a jacket on a chair. He can't help silently sympathizing with the builders. And, for the first time, his wife's fieriness frightens him.

He calls my aunt Kata, and my mother, sister and I spend the last week of the house renovations at Kata's house in Surrey. The builders, assured that they won't have to face my mother any more, come back and finish the job.

My mother has taken her first tiny step away from the world.

31

More connections appeared in unexpected places. I met a dozen strands of my past, traces of different journeys and places and people, in a single Elizabeth David recipe. It was in my mother's fragile, overused copy of *Spices, Salt and Aromatics in the English Kitchen*, Elizabeth David's exhaustive exploration of how British colonialism brought back the joys of Indian and other Asian cooking to English cooks.

I came across the recipe when I was planning what to make for dinner one night. My friend Richard Poureshagh was coming, bringing his new girlfriend, Donna, for the first time. Two days earlier an old family friend, Arthur Kellas, had died. Arthur and his wife, Bridget, were our direct next-door neighbours in Ardnamurchan. Which is to say they lived half a mile away along the barren headland in their own log house, with their own view of the Inner Hebrides. Their house was packed full of treasures from their lives overseas, many of them from Iran, where they had met when Bridget was the British ambassador's daughter and Arthur a young diplomat. Later they had returned for another tour of duty in Iran. I would often think of them when on reporting visits to Tehran. So Iran was on my mind as I was thinking about what to make for Richard and Donna – especially because with Richard there was a further Iranian connection.

His mother was a Scot, his father Iranian. No supporters of the Islamic Revolution, they fled Iran in 1979. Richard came to my school in Edinburgh that year, armed with one sentence in English: 'Where is the toilet?' When we were seventeen he had a girlfriend named Isabel. I had Clara. One evening Richard's mother, who had learned Persian cooking during her years in Tehran, cooked for the four of us, tactfully leaving the room after serving the food. What she left behind was a big dish of the most perfect Persian rice and a bowl of fesenjan – or fessanjun, or fezanjan, depending on one's transliteration. It was one of the most delicious things I had ever eaten – a stew (koresht, in Farsi) of ground walnuts, pomegranate juice, spices and chicken. Richard and I spoke of the dish and the meal often in the years to come. I had it only one other time, at Bridget Kellas's table in Ardnamurchan.

When I first started to visit Iran as a reporter, I hunted it down. I had a couple of mediocre ones in a restaurant across the street from the old American embassy. Eventually, my lovely translator Haleh's mother made me a proper fesenjan. What a combination of elements. The sweet-tart deep-red pomegranate juice mixed into the smooth nuttiness of the dark, mildly spiced sauce – a tinge of cinnamon and cardomom, perhaps some turmeric – and the whole thing folded over the meatballs Haleh's mother had made instead of chicken.

It was a dish of mothers. Still, no harm in trying to emulate them.

So this night I decided to cook it for Richard and Donna – as a surprise for him, a small, silent allusion, which I knew he would pick up, to dining with sweethearts now and twenty years before. I searched for a recipe. Haleh had, years earlier, given me a book of Persian recipes. I looked there and found a fesenjan recipe – but it included aubergine. That threw me. I had never had aubergine in fesenjan. So I looked online and found some alternatives that seemed more like it. I began to plan my shopping trip.

Later that day I stood in the kitchen and picked *Spices, Salt and Aromatics in the English Kitchen* off one of the bookshelves above the radiator where I had put most of my mother's cookery books. I wanted to see what Elizabeth David had to say about different ways of preparing rice in Asia. As I flicked through the pages, my eye caught something. I couldn't believe it – a recipe for 'Fezanjan', on page 204. It suggested duck rather than chicken or meatballs, but otherwise it was pretty much the same – the walnuts, spices and pomegranate juice, the key three ingredients, were there. And at the foot of the recipe, a note: 'Source: Mrs Arthur Kellas, British Embassy, Teheran. A well-known Persian delicacy'. And then a further source, below that: 'The Tenth Muse, Sir Harry Luke, 1954'. Which, I quickly found out, was subtitled 'A Gourmet's Compendium', and seemed to be the collected culinary curios of a mid-century British aristocrat. Bridget must have met him or heard his call for recipes and sent him her fezanjan. And Elizabeth David had lifted it in its entirety from Sir Harry, as she often did with writers she respected.

(Later, and shortly before she too died, Bridget related in a letter the full story, which involved yet another passing-on of the recipe: 'Harry Luke was visiting Tehran when we were there in our second innings. He came to supper with us and we dished up fesanjan, prepared by our wonderful old cook, Ahmad, who used to time his cooking by how long he would take when chanting verses from the Koran. Anyway, Sir Harry must have enjoyed the dish, because he later asked me for the recipe. I wrote down what Ahmad told me and submitted it, and so it went into print! Even though I had never actually made the dish myself. What a fraud I feel!')

I smiled at the circularity, then cooked with a sense of seren-dipity. When I was a teenager and for a few years managed to convince myself that there was a God, I warmed to Coleridge's pantheism, the sense of God being in nature, being everywhere, literally and physically as well as spiritually: 'one Life within us and abroad, Which meets all motion and becomes its soul ...' I would look at the sky and the sea and the land in Scotland and feel that things would hold together, that beyond the disintegration of what had meant everything in the first ten years of my life – my family – was something bigger and stronger and, unlike my family, unbreakable. I had not felt that about God for many years. But the hunger for connections had stayed. To me, food was appearing in everything, holding things together, linking me to my mother, overlapping with my past and my future; in this case, a single recipe was forging connections between my dear friend, a meal we had shared as teenagers, mothers in Iran and Scotland, and a dead cookery book writer I had never met but loved as if she were an aunt – a crotchety, demanding, lovable relative who bound us all together in my kitchen.

Richard came and, may his own mother forgive him, said that my fesenjan – Bridget's, Ahmad's, Sir Harry's, Elizabeth David's – was as good as his mum's.

∽

Fesenjan

This takes about an hour and a half. For the meat, you can use boneless chicken, duck or lamb meatballs. I've read that Iranians sometimes use pheasant. The whole thing is cooked in one large pot and serves about four people. The only thing you need to do some specialized shopping for is the pomegranate syrup or molasses or juice. Of these, juice is a bit of a Plan C but it's fine. The syrup is pretty easy to find in Middle Eastern groceries.

Heat up some oil or butter in the pot. Cook enough chicken pieces for four – four breasts, cut into quarters perhaps – until they're a nice brown colour. Take them out with tongs and put them on a plate to one side.

Thinly slice a couple of onions and throw them in over a low heat so that they become all melty and sweet. You can experiment with turmeric, cardamom and cumin at this stage,

190

perhaps dropping a few pinches of whichever spice takes your fancy into the onions. Cinnamon too, if you want, although I wouldn't overdo the sweetness factor, given that you still have sugar and pomegranate to come. Nor do you want it too curry-ish, so go easy with the cumin. The spices in this dish, if you use them at all, should be faint melodies, not power chords.

Take a couple of handfuls of walnuts and whizz them in the food processor or blender. 'About the walnuts,' Bridget Kellas wrote to me:

> I found it made a difference how finely they were chopped or ground. When passed through my little old nut or cheese mill it made a very velvety sauce. Chopped, however small, in the Magimix the sauce is grittier or heavier. I once had fesenjan with a Bakhtiari family near Dizful in Khuzistan in a small mud house. The great matriarchal lady who prepared it was formidable (I have a sketch I made of her – I am proud of this drawing). Anyway, that fesanjan was exceedingly Gritty, Black, Sharp and Heavy. They had no means of chopping the walnuts in a Magimix – and the sauce must have been made with pom syrup: 'shireh'. This is wonderful stuff if you can find it (and useful in many ways). It is sometimes available at Greek or Middle Eastern shops.

Throw the walnuts in the pot, along with the chicken and 500 ml of stock or water. Bring this to the boil and then cook it gently, with the cover on, for up to half an hour.

At this point, tip in a couple of tablespoons of sugar, some salt and pepper and the magic pomegranate syrup. It's tempting to use masses but about 100 ml should do.

Cook it for another fifteen minutes or so, until the chicken or other meat is just right. Taste the sauce while it's bubbling away. If it's too sweet you can add a squeeze of lemon. Too tart and a bit more sugar will do the trick.

Persian rice is the crucial accompaniment for this. And perhaps a salad.

32

Surely somewhere in my mother's papers I would come across something kind and creative, some sign of her intelligence and gifts before things went wrong in her head. I was finding it tough going, all the raving poetry and polymath scribblings.

And then they began to appear.

I found more letters among the files relating to her teaching – one from the headmistress (a nun) at a Catholic school in London, dated November 1965. It was a letter of recommendation for my mother, who had clearly just completed her teaching practice at the school: 'She has a very pleasant manner with children and was popular with them while here', writes Sister Placidus, in looping blue ink. 'Mrs McAllester has personally much to give others and imparts the knowledge of her subjects, French and English, in an attractive way.'

Next out of the suitcase was a letter from the Hamlyn Group, a publisher, dated 20 October 1967. Fifteen days after my sister, Jane, was born. My mother's first child. 'Of course there is no hurry for the translation – as long as it is coming – and please don't worry about it', writes Christine Gray, of the Natural History Books department. 'What sort of baby is it? After your mentioning so much about it I am dying of curiosity.'

It was the first I knew that my mother had translated books for a living. An earlier letter from a different editor makes it clear that she was translating from the French volumes of an encyclopedia entitled *Colour Library of World Wildlife*. 'Ken Denham and I are very satisfied with the translation work you have done for us so far', writes the editor, 'and I understand that you will be able to do some more for us.' She was to be paid four guineas per thousand words.

And then I found a pink foolscap folder. In my mother's handwriting, in the top left-hand corner, was written in pencil: 'Cordon Bleu. Ann McAllester. 15 Ashworth Road, W9. 01 286 0689'.

I opened up the folder, which had been held together with a gob of Blu-tack, now almost as hard as clay. Inside were dozens of pieces of paper, written out on a typewriter and annotated by hand. Recipes. All of them classic French food. Some held together with now rusty staples. 'Gâteau au Chocolat Chantilly'.

'Carré d'Agneau Perinette'. ('For 4. Do not make stuffing too wet & soft,' my mother had scribbed in pencil at the top. 'Do not overcook garnish,' she had written at the end of the recipe. I wondered if she was taking notes in class or commenting on her own mistakes at home, warning herself off these missteps for future meals.)

Near the top of the pile was a piece of paper with her name written in the top left-hand corner. And typed out: 'Wednesday Morning and Afternoon – Advanced. May 3rd, 1972. Summer Term, 1972'. Below that title, a list of a dozen menus. A repertoire of classic French cuisine. My mother had, it seemed, decided that Elizabeth David and her other mentors – Robert Carrier, Katie Stewart – were not quite enough. She had to learn at the most famous of all cookery schools, Le Cordon Bleu.

I called the school. They dug out from their archives a card with her name on it, showing that she'd taken twelve advanced classes that spring and summer. Another small trace of my mother, left in a box file in a cookery school in Marylebone for thirty-five years. It was a year after she had blown up at the Irish builders, a year after my father first saw something different in his wife.

Some of the recipes she learned at Le Cordon Bleu were, I have to say, not the kind of food I really wanted to master: pineapple jelly salad (underlined, worryingly, in an approving way); devilled egg mousse; chicken with fruit salad (I'm not making this up). But most of them looked amazing, old-fashioned, intimidating. And irresistible. The only question was: which would I choose to master?

33

Now that I've thought about it some more, I see it was not the man who walked off the platform in the Boston subway who gave me my first scent of unexpected death and its sickly sweet, destructive, fascinating power. It came much earlier, from my mother.

My mother wants to further her career as a schoolteacher and has been accepted for a course at Moray House teaching college in Edinburgh. But there's a problem with the staff at the college, she confides to my father.

'They're spying on me,' she tells my father when they are alone. 'They have sent people up to Ardnamurchan even.'

'I don't think so, Ann,' he says. 'I doubt they'd do that.'

'I'm telling you, Don, they have spies watching me. All the time.'

There is nothing my father can do to persuade her that the staff at the teaching college she is yet to attend are not spying on her. As the days go by, her conviction hardens.

On 25 April 1981, my father's brother, Jim, calls from Birkenhead, near Liverpool, where my father grew up. My father is in the kitchen constructing bench seats out of wood when the phone rings.

'Don, Dad has died,' Jim says.

In the week that precedes the funeral, my father realizes that my mother is in no state to come with him to Birkenhead. I am eleven and my sister is thirteen. Mum will stay in Edinburgh with us. He drives very quickly south, down the M6 motorway, buries his father, stays three nights, and early on the Sunday morning after the funeral gets into the yellow Vauxhall estate and drives north, heading home. It is 3 May 1981. He's passing near a town called Abington when he feels an overwhelming need to pull the car over. Immediately. He sits in the car with his hands on the beige steering wheel, other cars racing past him along the tarmac of the A702 north. 'Something is very wrong,' he says to himself. 'Something has happened.'

He breathes in, turns the ignition key, and pulls out on to the main road.

Early the same morning, I open my eyes and look sleepily around my bedroom at the walls that are coloured somewhere between salmon pink and peach – my choice. My duvet is yellow, with white shapes like flowers. I roll over and stare at the weave of the grey carpet. I can hear my mother moving through the house in my half dreams. None of us usually gets up this early on a Sunday. I close my eyes and drift.

'Jane, Matthew.' It is my mother's voice from the ground floor.

My sister and I sleep in bedrooms on the second floor. I open my eyes again. 'I'm going out for a bit. I'll be back later.'

'OK, bye,' we call out, and we keep our heads on our pillows and begin to sink back into sleep.

Our mother opens the glass-panelled inner door and then the solid wood main door, and she walks down the flagstone path my father has laid in a deliberately crooked line through the front garden. The blue Mini is parked across the street, near the bank on the corner. She gets in, pulls away from the kerb, and begins to drive through Edinburgh, the city where she grew up and met my father and then came back to in 1973 after their years in London.

She drives past the elegant Georgian architecture of the New Town and keeps going east, until she reaches the volcanic

196

hill known as Arthur's Seat, jutting out of the city. It's a place where people park their cars and go for short walks to take in the panoramic view of the city and the North Sea. She keeps driving and heads south, toward the King's Buildings, a campus that is part of the University of Edinburgh. She knows the city well, knows where she can find some solitude on a Sunday morning.

Her first home in Edinburgh, after her family moved back from London after the Second World War, was a house on Blackbarony Road, which leads out on to the King's Buildings.

She lived there until she was sixteen. Nearby are the crags and gorse and woodland of Blackford Hill, another of Edinburgh's many semi-wild, often deserted parklands. This is where she played as a child and where she has taken us for a Sunday afternoon walk a hundred times.

When she was a child it was an excellent place to play hide-and-seek. There was a small farm nearby, with chickens and horses. In those days, the quarry was a distant, largely deserted place. When she takes us to Blackford Hill, we bring stale bread in brown paper bags to throw towards the ducks and swans and moorhens on the pond.

Blackford Glen Road is narrow and runs alongside a stream next to the campus. She turns up the road and drives as far as she can, to a deserted car park. She turns the engine off and sits in the Mini, her husband driving home from his father's funeral, her children asleep at home. And she swallows all the pills she has brought with her. Before long she is unconscious, drifting away from her unbearable sadness for what she believes will be the last time.

The fire brigade has a Sunday morning exercise scheduled at the secluded Blackford Quarry, near the rough ground where my mother has parked. One of the firemen notices a woman slumped over in the blue Mini.

'Do you know where Mum went to?' I ask Jane. We are in the living room upstairs, the TV room. It's on, but there's nothing much good to watch on a Sunday morning. Some hymns. I feel restless anyway.

'No,' she says. 'She'll be back soon.' This is an assertion from my older sister, not a statement of fact, and I pick up on the difference, but I say nothing. In the absence of Mum or Dad, when we can't reach either of them and don't know exactly where either of them is, Jane assumes a sudden authority in my eyes.

Our mother has not left a message on the green plastic tablecloth. Always, she scribbles a note there if she's going out for a bit. She tells us when she'll be back and where she's gone. She never leaves for more than fifteen or twenty minutes.

We wait a bit longer and look out the window, hoping to see her Mini pull up. Or Dad in the Vauxhall. It's hard to concentrate on a game or a book. I pick up my white rugby ball and throw it in the air, spinning it around on its axis, catching it and turning my shoulder into the onrushing opposite team's players. And I go to look out the window again for Mum or Dad.

No one comes.

Eventually a car does pull up outside our front gate. It is a police car. We look down from the window, stepping back a little so that we won't be seen by the policeman walking up the crooked path.

The bell rings. We are scared of policemen. They have the power to lock people up. Are we in trouble? Are they going to put us in jail?

My sister goes to the door. I remain a few steps up the staircase.

'Miss McAllester? Can I come in for a moment?' the policeman asks.

We have been drilled not to let strangers into the house, but my sister decides that you don't say no to a policeman. Two of them are soon standing in the hallway.

'Your mother has taken a few too many pills,' the policeman

says, after he has ascertained that our father is out of town. He is dressed all in black, apart from his white shirt. 'Is there anyone you could call to come and take care of you?'

My sister calls Fi, the mother of my friend Mike. When Mike and his mum arrive, Mike asks me if I'm OK. I start to sob and, like grown men or brothers, we hug. I don't really understand what is going on, but I know that for the first time in my life my mum is not able to look after me.

My father arrives at the house. He has carried with him, since Abington, the same roadside conviction that something is wrong. He opens the front door and walks in to the hallway. It is empty.

'Hello?' he calls out. 'Ann?' A note on the kitchen table from Fi tells him that my sister and I are at her house.

In the emergency room of the Royal Infirmary, my mother is unconscious. She has her stomach pumped. She is put in a locked ward. After some days she comes home. My father does not ask her too much about what she has done, but he is sure that it was not a cry for help: his wife wanted to die.

She is clearly not well yet. Her paranoia and delusions and sadness have survived the quarry and the hospital. She goes, for the first time, to a psychiatric hospital.

My father drives us there in the sunshine of an early-summer afternoon. We sit on a wooden park bench on the lawn of the hospital, surrounded by trees. My mother speaks quietly and smiles. She seems less alert, less alive, as if she is not entirely paying attention to us. She holds our hands until we leave and stays in the hospital for weeks.

'The last few nights I spent in the hospital I slept in a room with only three beds in it,' she writes in a six-page story called 'Portrait of a Mad Woman'. I found it in her papers and have changed some of the names.

There was me, Christine and Lucy. Lucy was about my age, a slender, pretty girl who has never married and felt that she had failed as a woman because she had no husband and no child. She had been a theatre sister in [a hospital in Scotland], but would never work as a nurse again, we knew. The media had been making a meal of the trial of the Yorkshire Ripper; there had been a great deal of talk about schizophrenia, about 'voices': during this time Lucy had hidden away from the rest of the ward, as though she were afraid that we would blame her for his atrocities, or as though she blamed herself. She was schizophrenic. She had spoken to me one day as we sat on a bench in the sun, smoking and drinking Nescafé.

'I am mad, you know.'

'So am I.'

She smiled, and told me that she had often been a patient in this hospital; that once she had been in a locked ward for a year: we both looked to the main hospital building, to the top storeys where the locked wards are, wards from which some people do not emerge until they are dead, wards from which we sometimes heard strange, frightening sounds. I could not imagine neat, gentle Lucy up there, locked in ...

We all three cried, the day I left the hospital. To Christine I left my make-up, for her to play with; to Lucy, a begonia in flower that my sister had brought me from England, for her to care for. I think they wept because I was going home to a husband and children, to my home. Perhaps they wept because they would miss me. They were without envy: I felt ashamed to have so much that they did not have, would not have, yet in neither of them did I ever detect the unmistakable whiff of jealousy. Curious, yes, and full of wonder.

'Is that your husband?'

'Are those your children?'

'Aren't they beautiful?'

I said I would come back, that the three of us would go out together, that we would go to the beach.

It was summertime.

When my mother comes home, she seems calm and happy. But my sister and I notice that our mother has odd gaps in her memory. She cannot, for example, remember the previous Christmas. How is that possible? Christmas is the family's most elaborate, most anticipated annual celebration. She had prepared for weeks, as she always does. I had gone with her for one of my favourite days of the year, the Christmas food shopping trip. To Herbie's deli to buy the whole Stilton, the sample passed over the counter to me on a knife, the mould-veined cheese melting and bubbling in my mouth. To the butcher, where the green and white and russet pheasants hung in pairs around the walls, to order the ham for Christmas Eve and the turkey for Christmas Day. To the greengrocer, where I could choose which kind of satsumas – the ones with loose peels and no pips, always – to carry away in a whole box. To the supermarket, Safeway, where for the only time in the year we were allowed to walk down the sweets aisle and help ourselves to its treasures, filling the trolley up with Rose's, Dairy Milk, Chocolate Oranges and bars of Bournville. In another aisle I could pick out the biggest box of Twiglets, my favourite things in the world – crispy wheat sticks covered in Marmite-like brown stuff. And finally, the greatest treat, the straight-faced visit to a grown-ups' shop, Oddbins. The booze shop. I stood on the wooden floor and gazed up at the towers of red and green bottles, knowing that one day I could drink what they held and become as happy as my parents and other grown-ups did when they poured wine and whisky and beer into glasses I could only look at now. That was my favourite stop because it was full of far-off promise. For the rest, I would only have to wait a week or so. Then the feasting could begin.

On Christmas Day, the four of us – and guests whom I no longer remember – had sat around the black-painted oak table and eaten our way through smoked salmon, melon, prosciutto, turkey, a hundred roast potatoes, home-made chocolate and strawberry ice creams and Christmas pudding with brandy butter. We had laughed and pulled Christmas crackers and watched a James Bond film afterwards.

'What did we eat?' my mother asks me.

'You don't remember?'

'No.'

'You did your strawberry ice cream. It was so good. Do you remember what presents you got?'

'No, Matty, I don't remember a thing,' she says. She is not angry. She seems a little sad that she can't remember Christmas, but she is calm. 'They gave me some pills in the hospital and it affected my memory.'

My mother has forgotten a lot of things. She is quieter and doesn't seem to have as much energy as she had before she went into hospital. She puts less effort into cooking, and I notice that her food isn't as good as it once was. In fact, it is sometimes bland. Fried lamb chops and boiled potatoes and frozen peas, sitting on a cold plate. Baked beans from a tin begin to make more regular appearances. Bacon sandwiches. Frozen pizzas. Frozen reconstituted turkey steaks. Frozen chips, warmed up in the oven on the same baking tray as the turkey steaks.

She sits next to me on the bench as I eat one of her meals, poking the fried, unseasoned pork belly around the greasy plate. She's also cooked some boiled potatoes and frozen French beans. I don't complain, but there is no joy in the eating.

'Is that good?' she asks me.

'It's fine,' I say, not very generously. But perhaps no other change in my mother is as much of a shock to me as this dramatic downgrading of her cooking.

'I've totally forgotten how to cook, you know,' she says, matter-of-factly. 'I know I used to know how to cook, but I don't remember a single recipe. That all went away in the hospital. And I'm not really interested in cooking any more.'

The rind on the pork belly is chewy, not crispy. I cut it off and swallow the tepid, milk-coloured meat.

Some weeks later she goes back to hospital. And when she comes home she is even calmer than before. For a while.

In her story about being in hospital, my mother describes a day after she was discharged when she took Christine to the botanical gardens in Edinburgh. The story ends like this:

I took Christine back to the hospital and left without going in. I said I would phone and arrange for us to go to the beach with Lucy. Christine wanted to go to the beach: she had never been to the beach and asked me to describe it and to tell her what we could do there. She could not understand what I told her. I did not know how to tell her of the long waves and the seagulls, of the wind along the sand and the islands out there in the mist.

As I drove away I began to shake, in my stomach. I had not realized how tense I had been, being with Christine, how much more mad she had seemed to me that day when I no longer shared her hospital life, how frightened I had been in the glass-houses lest she might suddenly become wild and destructive, how frightened I was of taking her to something as powerful as the sea. I was afraid of being alone on the beach with my two friends, Christine and Lucy. My own madness was too recent, too raw a wound that they might reopen. I was afraid for myself and so I let Christine down; I did not fulfil my promise to take her to the beach. That was cruel. I joined all those other people who should have looked after Christine but did not, or could not.

The Hall of Mirrors at a fair in Scotland

34

My mother's medical history cost me fifty pounds. Ten for the fee, forty for the photocopying. In mid-November 2007, after weeks of my waiting and emailing and phoning, the medical records had moved from whatever building they were kept in by the local authority to my mother's former doctor's surgery, which happened to be a five-minute walk from my house. I slid the cheque under the glass window and the office manager passed me a large brown envelope, which I carried back up past the pawnshops and hardware shops and bookmakers of Kilburn High Road and along the street to my home. It was a Friday afternoon, and I was working to a deadline with a magazine article. And then I was due to go to Spain on Sunday for another magazine.

'I don't have time to look right now,' I told myself, throwing the thick envelope on to my desk.

Moments later I slid my finger under the flap of the envelope and opened it up.

My eyes raced over the pages, flicking through, reading letters from psychiatrists and handwritten doctors' notes. After an hour I picked up the whole pile of A4 paper and slid it back inside the envelope, where it stayed for a month while I wrote about anything other than my mother – Somali gangs in Minneapolis, obscure crustaceans that attach themselves to the coastal rocks of Galicia. And I cooked. Christmas was coming. The envelope sat on a stool under an increasingly large pile of newspapers, magazines and paperwork.

35

I began to read and plan and make lists on blank sheets of A4 paper a month before Christmas. Lists of remembered dishes, family recipes, ingredients I would have to find, nibbles I would leave lying around the house as they used to be every Christmas in our house. I would pickle onions, bake my first Christmas cake, steam my first Christmas pudding, whip up my first brandy butter, roast my first turkey, make my mother's impossibly creamy chocolate ice cream for the first time, and give Pernilla a sense of what our Christmases had been like. I had not made Christmas for her before. In my mother's recipe book, which I approached for the first time since I had gone hunting for the ice cream recipe, I found two handwritten recipes for Christmas cake – 'Sister Agatha's Christmas Cake' and another copied out from a newspaper. In Katie Stewart's *Times Cookery Book*, which would have fallen into a hundred sections if I had not cupped it delicately in my hand, I found the chocolate ice cream. Pickled onions may not have been particularly Christmas food, but we had made them every year, standing around in the kitchen peeling shallots by the dozen and letting the tears roll down our cheeks, laughing at the acidic stinging in our eyes.

As I made my lists, I was surprised to find myself suddenly hesitating over the idea of recreating my mother's food. I had not expected this reluctance just as I was preparing to produce in my own home the meal of all the year's meals, the meal that had once showcased my mother's talents and our appetites, the meal that had bound us together for so many years.

Pernilla's mother and stepfather were coming all the way from Vancouver. Her stepbrother, his wife and their baby would be here. My sister was coming, as were two friends – a brother and sister. This was my chance to piece together the sort of big family meal and celebration my mother used to make the focal point of our year. It was just that, well, this was my meal, not hers. I began to feel that I wanted her with me, yes, but I did not want her running the show. Meals are a source of life, not an echo of death, and while I still needed to capture my young mother's sense of joy in cooking for her family, I did not want to produce a morbid, perfect re-enactment of a feast from a time long past. I wanted to use some of my own cookery books, some of the recipes I had found in food magazines and newspapers, some of the ideas I had been forming during my months of teaching myself to 'cook properly', as she saw it.

I wanted a lemon granita to take the edge off the heavy sweetness of ice cream and fruit cake and steamed fruit pudding with brandy butter. Not to forget the mince pies my sister would be bringing. Or the gingerbread men my mother-in-law would bake. I wanted to bake airy, irresistible gougères to serve as people waited to eat. I wanted a light, slightly surprising starter, and I had found a recipe for a salad of sushi-grade tuna, seared and coated in poppy seeds and sweet paprika, on a bed of leaves and segments of clementine, drizzled with a clementine vinaigrette. I had found an Italian-style turkey recipe in a Thanksgiving issue of *Gourmet* magazine, and I wanted to make its Italian sausage stuffing and its lemon butter, sliding the butter between the skin and the breast of the bird, a trick I knew well with chicken. I wanted to liven up my Brussels sprouts with small chunks of pancetta and chestnut. I wanted to glaze my carrots with cider, drizzle maple syrup over my roasting parsnips and mix port and orange juice into my fresh cranberry sauce. I wanted to wrap the chipolata sausages with slithers of fatty Italian pancetta, not slices of British bacon.

My mother never did any of that.

But I imagined she would approve of how I had learned to cook in my own way, moving quickly around the kitchen, cooking some things days in advance, timing the full eighteen dishes that were going into this meal so that on Christmas Day they would emerge smoothly from the kitchen and I would still have time to talk to the guests. Perhaps I still needed the book open, perhaps I still could not cook properly, as she saw it, but I was disappearing into my cooking, closing off the world so that my family could celebrate.

Besides, in talking with my aunt Kata, a rather different version of my mother's cooking had emerged. 'She always had her cookery book open,' my aunt told me.

'No,' I said, 'that surely can't be true – she told me over and over again that it wasn't proper cooking unless you had the book closed.'

'No,' Kata said forcefully, 'she always used the cookery book to do anything.'

'Oh, I see,' I said.

On Christmas Day I woke up with a brutal dose of flu, cooked through the morning, could barely hear what anyone was saying, and had to lie down for a stretch during the meal. I have no idea what anything tasted like.

ℐ

Cranberry Sauce with Port, Orange and Cloves

I've adapted this from a recipe I found in the Thanksgiving issue of *Gourmet*, American's most beautiful and inspiring food magazine. Cranberry sauce is one of those things that, if it comes from a jar or a tin, will ruin a turkey. A good cranberry sauce makes even people who are bored with turkey perk up a little bit. It's very simple, takes no time, and you can do it days in advance and keep it in the fridge.

Gourmet uses tangerines rather than oranges, and I've thrown in the cloves. My guess is that you could really experiment with this in other happy ways. Cointreau or triple sec instead of port? Or fino sherry? A little candied ginger? Or some grated fresh ginger? But nothing that overwhelms the fresh cranberries.

In a pan, simmer about a half a kilo of fresh cranberries, 150 g of sugar, 100 ml of port, two cloves and a good bit of orange zest. Simmer until the sugar has melted and keep it going for another ten minutes or so. Most of the cranberries will have burst but don't cook it so much that they lose all their shape and the whole thing becomes a mush. Then let it cool. Pick out the cloves and throw them away.

36

With Christmas and its flu over, I sat down with the pile of photocopies that had been waiting for me on my desk for a few weeks. The first document in my mother's medical records was a typed letter from an optician to my mother's doctor. 31 October 1974. It describes a check-up. 'She has no complaints whatever as far as her eyes are concerned and on examination I found her vision to be normal,' the optician writes.

The banalities of medical bureaucracy don't last long. In November 1978 her doctor conducted a physical examination. There are notes about her parents. Her father: 'Depression @ 60 (E.C.T. treatment)'. Her mother: 'Formerly alcoholic – now T.T. [teetotal]'. There are a few hints. The doctor writes of her being 'uneasy about readiness to take drink, which has a stimulating effect, making her argumentative. She has no association with a church now, and sometimes feels guilty … Would like more children but husband unwilling and both feel it is now a bit late … Tense emotionality, probably ordinarily heightened.'

And then came a letter from a professor of psychiatry to her doctor, written on 8 June 1981.

'The above was admitted on 5th May, after I had myself earlier seen her in the Poisons Unit at the Royal Infirmary,' the professor writes.

You will remember that there is a very strong family history of mental illness … At the time of admission and for the subsequent ten days the patient was extremely depressed and was preoccupied with a number of paranoid ideas, feeling that an arrangement had been made between her own brother, Moray House and some people in the Highlands to put her to the test in some way by depicting her life and feelings in front of her when she had been away on a brief holiday recently in the Highlands. We had thought of giving the patient ECT, but persisted with [the anti-depressant] amitriptyline, and after a couple of weeks on 200 mg nightly she made an excellent recovery and has gone home.

I found another letter written by one of the professor's staff to another doctor at the hospital, recording more details of my mother's admission.

Thank you for taking this lady. She took a mixed overdose of drugs while sitting in her car in a quarry. She had earlier driven to Arthur's Seat where she wanted to find a beautiful place in which slowly to die ... In recent weeks the patient has become increasingly depressed and has had a number of ideas of reference. She feels that people look at her and that if they were speaking about her they would be saying that she is a failure who has let down her family and her husband.

The family went to the Highlands a couple of weeks ago for a few days' break and when she came back she felt that the whole trip had somehow been arranged in every detail with special reference to herself. She has had difficulty sleeping at night and has felt her thoughts going round and round on unhappy themes. She has been thinking about how to kill herself. On the day preceding the overdose she went round to see her father but she felt somehow that he and her brother ignored her. Then she went to the cinema with a friend and had wanted to go to a cheerful picture but her friend insisted on going to see *Ordinary People*. The next day the patient made an attempt to kill herself.

212

I wasn't expecting to laugh out loud while reading this stuff. Robert Redford and his Oscar-winning family glumfest – it was all too much for my mum. If only she had gone to see *Private Benjamin*. (Although these things are all in the eye of the beholder: Mark David Chapman found *Ordinary People* to have a calming effect, and it dissuaded him from killing John Lennon on his initial visit to New York in 1980.)

And so that was the real beginning of the story that the huge pile of paper told. From 5 May 1981, the letters and notes came regularly.

Her anti-depressants worked for a few months, and both she and my father were hugely relieved that the worst was over. But by December of that year, the month that was always the happiest and most food-laden in my world, she was wobbling badly.

I remembered her taking me to the GP once. I didn't remember what was wrong with me but it was nothing serious. 'Could you wait for me in the waiting room, please, Matthew?' she said, when the doctor had finished examining my stomach or ear or whatever was the cause of the visit. I sat in the small waiting room off the hallway, looking at an old copy of the *Radio Times*. She was in there for ten, perhaps fifteen minutes. I began to worry. The door finally opened. She was crying.

'Come on, Matthew,' she said. I followed her. She was rushing to the car.

'What's wrong?' I asked her when we were in the car.

'Nothing,' she said, still crying.

I didn't understand what was happening to my mum at all but it scared me.

In December she noted that her concentration had become more impaired, the doctor writes, that she was waking during the night and again had feelings of hopelessness and was contemplating suicide.

The doctor's notes made me picture her, standing in the kitchen stirring the dried fruit and brown sugar and butter in a mixing bowl, making yet another Christmas cake, ordering yet another turkey from the butcher, taking me to buy the crate of satsumas from the greengrocer and the whole Stilton from the deli, finding no comfort in this burdensome preparation for a feast she no longer cared about, sensing her old identity melting away like the chunks of chocolate she was heating in a mixing bowl that was sitting in a pan of boiled water. The chocolate ice cream had to be made.

But my memory offers a different picture: I don't remember anything but excitement and warmth.

Dominic and Uncle Paul come for Christmas dinner. Dominic is staying for several days, as he is travelling from his current home in Yorkshire – where he is caretaker on a country estate – to an island near Ardnamurchan. He has brought with him a brace of pheasants shot on the estate, and my mother and I hear shrieks and giggles and some rude words from the utility room off the kitchen as my father and Dom struggle to draw and pluck the birds, bolstering their efforts amid the guts and feathers with tumblers of Scotch. Having Dom and Paul there for dinner is a treat for Jane and me, and I remember no Christmas as fondly. But I know nothing of my mother's sleeplessness and desire to die.

Within a few days of that happy night, my father and Dominic drive my mother to the psychiatric hospital. 'The little electrical "gates" in my brain are malfunctioning, and that's what's causing the problems,' she explains to Dominic, very lucidly.

'She began a course of ECT on 30th December 1981, and when seen on 13th January 1982, after six treatments she appeared much brighter and said that she had not felt so well for many months,' a doctor writes.

I wonder why Mum is sad at Christmas and how anyone could get that fed up at the happiest time of the year, when there are piles of presents and that whole, impossibly creamy

Stilton to dig the long-handled spoon into, with no limits on the amount I am allowed to eat, because it will all go dry and the sides of the cheese will crack unless it is eaten quickly.

'She was discharged home on 27th January 1982 to continue on amitriptyline 150 mg at night.'

She comes home from hospital after being there for almost a month.

'Mum, will you come and play on the TV game with me?'

My favourite Christmas gift is one of the first generation of video games, a primitive console that lets you play basic forms of tennis, squash and football. I had roped her into playing game after game with me in the days immediately after Christmas, before she returned to hospital.

'This is fun,' she says, as if it's the first time she's played. She has no memory of playing the game before.

The medical notes, and my father's memory, record that time as one of improvement in her health. But by that stage their marriage was beyond repair.

It is a Saturday night, in early October 1982, and we have gone out to a Spanish restaurant. It is my sister's choice because it is her birthday meal. That's the way it works. On our birthdays, we get to choose our favourite food. Then at the weekend we can choose a restaurant. I always opt for the burger paradise that is Bell's Diner. Jane is fifteen and has more sophisticated tastes. She wants paella.

At the restaurant my mother whispers something aggressively to my father. I hear the words 'making eyes'. They are sitting opposite my sister and me. My father looks embarrassed.

'What are you saying, Mum?' I say. 'Don't you know it's rude to whisper at the table?'

'I was telling your father how the lady at the next table has clearly taken a shine to him. She's making eyes at your father. He's very handsome, so it's hardly surprising.'

I sense that my mother does not mean this as a compliment.

In the past couple of years I have heard this voice of hers, ever more frequently, ever more loudly. Sometimes I hear it at night, coming from the living room, rising in a crescendo that can't be hidden from my sister and me, as we lie in our beds behind closed doors. Sometimes it erupts in front of us. Once, it comes from the kitchen, and I hear the name of a woman I know and like very much and my mother is saying that this woman has been 'in my bed'. I know that my mother and father's bed is meant to be only for them.

The kitchen has, at times, come to seem less of a happy place than it once was. It was in the kitchen a couple of years before, when I was nine, that we had a family talk that changed our lives for a while, and not for the better. We were a family devoted to watching *Dallas*, every Wednesday evening at ten minutes past eight. So my father looked at Jane and me and reached out to Dallas, a place we all understood and shared, for help.

'Do you know how on *Dallas* sometimes J.R. has affairs?' he asked. I sat on one of our orange plastic chairs. I stared at the floor. Jane sat nearby.

'Yes,' I said, not liking where this was going.

'Yes,' Jane said, in a quiet, brave voice.

'Well, I've had an affair. But it's over now.'

'Who with?' I asked, knowing the answer already.

'That doesn't matter,' my parents said. But the affair clearly mattered to my mother, because my father explained that he would be moving out for a while to live with my mother's brother, Paul. He came back before too long because my mother missed him so much. I missed him more than I could say. And when he came back, he and my mother were happy again. But then came the spies from Moray House and the quarry and the hospital and her lingering anger at what my father had done.

*　　*　　*

When we get home from the Spanish restaurant, my father tells my sister and me that we need to have a family talk. We sit in the living room. It is Saturday night, the most fun evening of the week. But this is not fun. From past experience, I know that 'family talks' never are.

'As you probably know,' he says, 'Mum and I haven't been getting on very well. So I'm going to move out again.'

We are silent.

'How long for?' I ask. I will miss him while he's gone, but we've done this before and it didn't last long.

'We're not sure,' Dad says.

My mother erupts. 'Don, for God's sake, for once in your life can't you just tell the bloody truth?'

And that is the end of my family.

37

My father has moved out, and my mother is talking about a new start in a new house. After school one Friday in the spring of 1983, she and I go with an estate agent to see a new flat. I don't want to leave our house.

'Do you want to get those jeans?' she says as we leave, and I can't believe what I'm hearing. I am on a pretty strict allowance and I have to buy my own clothes and records, but now she's offering to buy me my first pair of Levi's 501s. We drive to Cockburn Street in Edinburgh's Old Town. After we have completed the jeans transaction, we walk past a record shop. I tell her that at my friend Mike's house I've been listening to the new single by David Bowie, 'Let's Dance'. I had always considered Bowie to be too weird, not very melodic. But there's something about this song that I really love.

'Come on,' she says, and takes my hand in an excited way, not an embarrassing Mum way, and we're going inside the record shop and she's buying me not just the 'Let's Dance' single but the whole album.

At home I sit on my bed, put my headphones on, and listen to the record. I save up to buy *Hunky Dory*, *Ziggy Stardust* and the 'Ashes to Ashes' seven-inch. 'My mother said, to get things done, you better not mess with Major Tom,' Bowie sings, and I have little idea what he's trying to say, if anything, but it thrills and comforts me more than anything I've heard before.

One day I read in the local paper that Bowie is coming to

Edinburgh to play a stadium show in the summer. My mother calls my father, who takes time off work to buy tickets. Their separation hasn't yet prevented them from coordinating good things for their children. I think they want to cheer us up with a treat or two. My mother's next call is to my teacher: 'Matthew will be leaving school early on Tuesday, June 28,' she explains. As usual, she is telling, not asking. She picks me up that afternoon, and, after we have parked the car, the two of us make our way through the tens of thousands walking to Murrayfield rugby stadium. Once at our seats we wait for hours, listening to two opening acts until the darkness falls and the lights finally dim and I stand on my seat to work out which of the men coming on to the stage is Bowie. And then it's clear – he's not there yet. Moments later, the blond, blue-suited Bowie finally appears onstage, and there's no mistaking him – he seems to glow. My patient, mildly interested mother stands beside me, smoking cigarettes and watching the show without knowing a single song. The rain begins to shower down on the 40,000 people there, nearly all of them older than me and younger than my mother. 'I could play the wild mutation as a rock 'n' roll star,' he sings in his opening song, and I think to myself that I've found a world through this music and this singer that offers me an escape, a way to change things. It feels like the most important day of my life. Within two years I have every record Bowie has ever made.

Years later, at a swanky party in an Upper East Side apartment full of famous artists and paintings by famous artists, I was helping myself to roast ham at the buffet table when I realized David Bowie was standing next to me, filling his plate. I scrambled for something to say: 'That ham looks really tasty', or 'Your music still provides me with a deep sense of comfort that will probably be with me for life'. I took a spoonful of potato salad and said nothing.

On 1 December 1983, my mother writes to her doctor explaining that she is divorcing my father. Her lawyers, she says, have asked her to ask her doctor for an account of her illnesses.

The doctor replies on 7 December. The letter reveals more details about her depression in the 1970s and beyond.

'She is a woman of education and intelligence, charming and fair-minded', he writes. 'In 1975 she required treatment when pressure from her parents provoked depression. In 1978 she found herself drinking excessively. In 1980 the couple had a temporary social separation and Mrs McAllester required treatment with mild tranquillizers. In 1981 she had further problems with her father and with her son, who had abdominal pain – a first symptom of development of behavioural difficulty later leading to problems at school.'

My own name seems to pop up now and then in my mother's records.

Some years later the same doctor writes: '8/5/86. Worried re. son's behaviour – Matthew (16) does not talk and has been violent to things @ home. Apparently OK @ school and elsewhere.'

I am elsewhere described as 'rude'.

38

If you walk out of our red sandstone terraced house, turn left at the front gate and head down the road, you come to a small group of shops clustered around one corner of a junction. There's Bob's, the barber, where my mother until recently has imposed such short haircuts on me that older boys at school call me Spike. I'm thirteen now, so my freedom to choose is growing, and I choose not to get haircuts that make me an object of ridicule.

Another shops sells newspapers, cigarettes, stationery, sweets and cheap toys. I have been negotiating the delicate transition with the old man in the shop from sweets buyer to pornography buyer, trying to look as though I have aged several years in the course of a few months. On the corner is Haddows, the off-licence. One of dozens of Haddows shops in Scotland, its sign is in white letters on a green plastic background. Haddows is where I usually go with Dad when he doesn't have time to go to a better wine shop. As of several months ago, he no longer lives with us, so I am no longer taken there.

It's a warm, late-summer Friday evening, and school is over for the day. Maroon-and-white double-decker buses belonging to the Lothian Regional Council churn past me as I walk to the corner and cross the road because I see my mother moving slowly from the shops, back to our house. She's carrying a green-and-white bag.

'Hi, Mum.'

'Hi, Matty.'

I put my hand out to pull open the plastic bag in her hands and she lets me.

'What's the whisky for?' I ask. There is a half-sized bottle of Bell's in there. Full bottles are what get poured when we have guests around, when Dad is having an evening whisky. I have never seen half bottles in the house. Half bottles are what my friends and I save up to buy every now and then when some-one's parents are away for the day – if anyone will sell to us. Half bottles are what the men who lie on the pavement drink. I have an urge to take the whisky away from my mother. I don't quite know why, but I know she shouldn't have it.

'Oh, it's nothing,' she says. 'Don't worry.'

We walk on in our different directions.

I know she is unhappy that she and Dad are getting divorced. She has been spending a lot of time in bed. She gets very angry at and about Dad. She takes sleeping pills.

'Do they completely knock you out?' I ask her hopefully.

'No,' she says, sensing my game. 'They tip me into sleep, that's all.'

I test this over the months and play very loud Bowie records to see if she'll wake up. When she doesn't, I quietly let myself out of the house into the summer evenings, and never once does she appear at the window to catch me moving quickly along the crooked garden path and out of sight.

My mother indulges me with another treat: I am allowed to have a black Labrador. It will not be the family's dog, it will be mine. I pick out the smallest from the litter at a farm outside Edinburgh on a hot summer afternoon, and I call her, of course, Ziggy. She is my solace and friend. When my mother drinks and cries and shouts, Ziggy and I go and hang out in my bedroom and I talk to her. She's pretty stupid but she's lovely. A year later, when I'm fourteen, my mother drives Ziggy and me in the Vauxhall to a cricket match I'm playing in. Ziggy, who could do with a little more training and discipline, is wriggling like a black seal in the back seat. It is a hot Saturday morning in May. After the long game, I walk back home in the evening through the park and along the wide avenues of north Edinburgh. My mother is sitting in the kitchen. She gets up from the wooden stool she's sitting on and puts her palms on my cheeks.

'Matty, I've done something terrible,' she says. For a second I am not alarmed, because she often does terrible things these days, usually to people she is supposed to love, usually in the form of vicious words. But this time she looks afraid of something.

'I left Ziggy in the car. She suffocated in the heat. She's dead.'

Inverockle, Ardnamurchan

39

'Mrs McAllister [*sic*] was brought up to hospital by her ex-husband on the 29th April [1985] on account of her mood disturbance and inability to carry out simple household tasks,' writes a doctor at the hospital.

'On the day of admission she rang him and said that she was going to Confession and asked him to look after the children. He wondered whether she was having a further episode of depression and when the children said that she was unable to prepare the meal he went to the family home and brought Ann to hospital.' My father moved back in with us until our mother returned from the hospital.

The doctor continues:

Ann said that she had been drinking a bottle of wine or sherry a day for at least a fortnight prior to admission and that she had been taking an excess quantity of sleeping tablets. Initially these were temazepam but then I understand they were changed on account of the restrictions on prescribing that hypnotic. The new hypnotic, whose name she cannot recall, made her 'Zombie-like'. On at least one occasion she took these sleeping tablets during the day.

On admission Ann was unkempt, preoccupied and muttering to herself. Her mood was labile; predominately she was tearful and low in mood but at times she would giggle and laugh inappropriately. She expressed bizarre ideas such as the belief that she could be pregnant and that the baby was a monster on account of the atom bomb.

This note sparked a memory. 'I'd like to have another baby,' my mother told me one day when I was about fifteen. 'I always wanted another baby.'

'Mum, you're a bit old,' I said. Not to mention no longer married and with no apparent interest in ever being married again, I could have added. But I had learned by then not to take much of what she said seriously.

The handwritten notes of the admitting doctor, a different physician, quote my mother: 'I feel awful, I'm awful, I achieve nothing, do nothing and bother everyone with my beastly phone calls.'

'Poor Don,' she is quoted as saying, 'I don't know how he puts up with me.'

The doctor notes:

Dazed-looking but quite responsive. Sat quite still in chair apart from picking at hands. Head bent most of time. Expression gloomy. Speech normal in form but content full of thoughts of worthlessness, guilt and desire to shut world out. Lies in bed to escape but thoughts crowd in. Ideas of Reference – convinced people talking about her all the time.

My mother was given medication, the letter from the hospital to her doctor continues.

Twenty-four hours later she was entirely normal, her behaviour was appropriate, her thinking coherent and her mood was euphymic [the doctor intends to say euthymic, which means the patient is normal and no longer depressed]. She was noted to have a slight tremor but no other evidence of physical symptoms of alcohol withdrawal. She remained well over the next 5 days and was therefore discharged on no medication, and we presume that the psychiatric disturbance on admission was due to alcohol and drug misuse.

They presumed? Well, they got that seriously fucking wrong, I thought, when I read the letter. Did they not read the notes that were in front of me now, more than a quarter of a century later? How could they not see what was clear to me, a fifteen-year-old boy, what was clear to all in the family, what had been clear to the doctors who had treated her at the same hospital in 1981? Not very far below her now full-blown alcoholism was an underlying illness, a severe depression. Insanity.

The doctor continues, says that she has advised my mother not to drink for several months, but said that 'thereafter I did not see why she couldn't resume social drinking'.

My God, I thought, what was the doctor thinking? How could she have been so stupid? Did she think my mother would calmly return to having an occasional glass of sherry at cocktail parties?

Being well-spoken and intelligent does not make you sane. I could tell from the letter that the doctor was impressed by my mother's recent decision to return to university, to study theology. 'Ann is a first-year student on a theology course at New College, which she greatly enjoys,' the doctor writes. But to me, my mother's newfound desire to learn Hebrew and ancient Greek so that she could read earlier versions of the Bible was a cause for worry, not a sign that she was putting her life back together. Religion had become just another context for her increasingly common delusions of grandeur.

The doctor's note provoked another memory: my mother's summer journey, in 1986, to Greece and Israel. She went on her own, a middle-aged, mentally unwell woman, travelling for weeks by train through Europe and then ferry to the countries of the Bible languages. She wanted to study in Jerusalem. She wanted to master Greek and Hebrew so that she could read the Bible in its most influential versions. In Jerusalem she stayed at a hostel run by nuns for foreign students, made some friends and travelled in the region, in a country I was to move to years later. After several weeks she ran out of money and called her father, asking him to wire her some more. My grandfather, surely knowing that the last thing he should do was to subsidize my mother's further loony travels, declined and she returned, angry that her plans had been foiled.

The letter finishes: 'I have arranged to see Mrs McAllister [sic] in 5 days time to ensure that there really is no depressive illness lurking in the background, since she has had two past admissions for this and has a very strong family history of depressive illness.' As far as my mother's medical records showed, the doctors now saw her as someone with what was primarily a drinking problem. How could they have decided that alcohol was the fundamental problem? I did not understand it at the time and, as I read further into the notes, I understood it less.

'When I saw her today', writes the same hospital doctor in July 1985,

> she was most reticent to discuss her problems. Finally she burst out crying and professed to be lonely and finding it difficult to cope with the problems of two adolescent children on her own. Matthew has been accusing her of ruining his life probably referring to the break-up of the family and Jane has been sitting her A-levels ... I could tell from the shape of Ann's face that she had been drinking again and she admits to one bottle of wine or sherry every evening when she feels at her worst, particularly if the children are out.

'I felt today as I always have that she is strained, nervous and unhappy,' the doctor writes in September of that year. 'I am sorry to say I feel I have helped Mrs McAllister [sic] very little.'

The doctor's tone is becoming more concerned and gentle. She is clearly at a loss. My mother was slipping away from everyone. Two years later: 'This 44-year-old married woman was admitted to ... hospital on 31.7.87 feeling depressed and ashamed and having drank 3 bottles of whisky in 3 days,' a different doctor, one of the professor's staff, writes on 31 August, a month after my mother's admission.

229

Her brother, who had come to visit her, brought her to the hospital ... She described sleepless nights and although her appetite became good when she was in hospital, she had neglected to feed herself beforehand and lost a little weight. She said she had felt like committing suicide recently but was unable to because of her children. There appeared to be no hallucinations or delusions and she was clearly a woman of high intelligence with some insight into her current stresses ... She recovered very quickly from her excess of whisky, but the medium and long-term prognosis must be guarded, since it has been very difficult to help her in the past.

There were letters from my mother to her doctor, begging his help in repairing the family. There was a letter from a hypnotherapist my mother saw to help her give up smoking – including a note of how she overslept and didn't make the second appointment. One doctor notes she was smoking sixty cigarettes a day.

'Thank you very much for your letter about this unfortunate lady,' writes the doctor from the professor's staff, on 10 December 1987.

I have been quite distressed by her recent apparent deterioration. She failed to attend one of my Out-Patient appointments and then mistook the time of the next one. She presented visibly shaking, unable to drink a cup of coffee with-out spilling it and talking garrulously of a cure for smoking ... It is very difficult for me to tell whether the drink problem is masking a hypomanic episode, however her condition did not warrant admission.

Hypomanic episodes are the periods when mentally ill people, especially those with bipolar disorder, become extremely talk-ative, creative, intellectually agile, angry, or otherwise very clearly overexcited.

40

I wait until my mother and I have both calmed down from our latest quarrel. I need her to understand that I'm not making a threat out of anger. We are in the kitchen.

'Mum, I want to go and live with Dad,' I say. 'I'm just not happy here. And I don't make you happy. It's better this way.'

In the days that follow, she cries and I feel guilty. With me gone and my sister at college, I know that she will be alone now. She asks me to stay.

Then she yells about my father: 'He's won now. He's got what he wanted. He's got all the money and he's got you and I have nothing. Nothing. Nothing.'

She bangs her fist hard on the dining table and then breaks out into desperate sobs. I tell her that it's not that I want to live with Dad – I just can't keep living with her.

I move into the small room at my father's mews house. There's no desk for me to do my homework. The room is too small, too integrated into the house, for me to hide in. My records, my stereo, my other things – there's not enough room here for the possessions that give me comfort. This is exactly why I wanted to live on my own. I knew living with my father wouldn't be much better, and in some ways it is worse. But I have no choice.

A few weeks go by and he can tell I'm not happy. We are sitting in his small kitchen at dinner one evening.

'I know it's really small in there, but I think we may have a solution soon,' he says. 'I've bought the house next door, and

I'm thinking we could knock a hole in the wall between them and you could have a bit more space there.'

I look at him. 'You're saying I'm going to have my own place? Next door?'

'Well, we have to wait until the guy who's renting it moves out in a few weeks, but then, yes, if you want, that's where we'll put you. It's not terribly pretty in there – extremely seventies and a bit dark – but it's a lot more spacious than here.'

I can't quite believe it. Many years later he tells me that he had been planning this for a while – he had seen the trouble brewing between Mum and me – but he did not want to lure me away. If I came of my own accord, fine. And if I came, he knew there would not be enough space in his house.

'Do you want to see it?' he asks.

We go round and knock on the door, and the guy living there lets us in. My new home-to-be has a shit-brown ancient bathroom suite, tatty old cream carpets, wooden panelling, a cheap kitchen and a classic seventies gas heater. It could do with some major work. I am euphoric. I have gone, in a few seconds, from being one of the most self-pitying boys at my school to perhaps the luckiest in all of Edinburgh.

When the tenant leaves, a builder comes and knocks a door between the two properties, and when my father and I get out of the car and go in to what is essentially now one house through two different front doors, we laugh. 'It's like the Beatles in *Help!*,' I tell him, 'the way they get out of the limo, go through four doors, and end up in one long house.'

We rig up an old Morse Code buzzer so that he doesn't have to come and get me every time it's dinner or someone has called for me or he wants to speak to me. Three buzzes for food. Two for phone. One for a chat. He is teaching himself to cook, using a book by his old *Let It Bleed* cake-maker, Delia Smith, which is rather morosely titled *One is Fun!* I'm allowed beer. Clara can stay the night. I can cook for friends in my own little kitchen – and increasingly for my father. I borrow his *One is Fun!* and on the days it's my turn to cook he gives me ten pounds for the ingredients but expects some change from it.

One Wednesday I decide to cook Delia's Chicken Breast with Preserved Ginger Sauce. I've done the Pork Chop with Apples and Cider and the Chicken Véronique a few too many times. The recipe calls for three different kinds of ginger – root ginger, preserved ginger and preserved ginger syrup. I have never even heard of preserved ginger and I search in Safeway and in two delicatessens for it until someone tells me to try the Chinese food shop. Success. The ginger comes in a beautiful little blue and white urn. It's a bit pricey but it's getting late and if I don't buy it here then I'm never going to find it elsewhere and there will be no dinner.

'Hi Dad,' I say, calling him at work. 'I found the preserved ginger.'

'Great,' he says. 'Where?'

'At the Chinese food shop. It was a bit expensive. Eight pounds, actually. In fact, you owe me a couple of quid for the rest of the ingredients.'

'What? You are joking, aren't you?'

'Uh, no.'

'Eight quid for some ginger. That's absolutely ridiculous.' He is profoundly unamused.

'I'm sorry,' I say. 'It comes in a very nice porcelain urn, though.'

He does not see the funny side of this.

'It had better taste bloody amazing.'

He gives me a copy of *One is Fun!* for Christmas.

There are rules, of course, in my new teenage playboy existence. I have to call if I'm going to be home past twelve or stay at someone's house. I have to clean my half of the house. But I have it pretty good.

My mother does not like coming here. She has become very aggressive towards my father and anyone she considers his friend. Sometimes she will come to the mews and kick and punch his front door, shouting obscenities. His answering machine fills up with dozens of messages from her in a few hours. One day she bursts into his boss's office and spits at him. When she comes over, my father locks the door between my place and his. It is not possible for them to have a civil relationship any longer. Even if he wanted to help her, he couldn't. To her, he is the enemy. She says terrible things about him to me. And she tells me she still loves him deeply.

Living alone now, my mother deteriorates further. With my sister at university in Oxford, my mother's parents dead, nearly all her friends alienated by her accusations and hostile letters and phone calls, the job of keeping an eye on her falls to my uncle Paul and to me. My mother has moved to a new house, where she still keeps rooms for my sister and me. I have a key.

I am home at the mews in the early afternoon of 18 May 1988, when a manager from Safeway calls my father, telling him that his wife is in the supermarket. She was in the checkout queue, he says, when she turned to the customer next to her and began insisting that she get to the hospital immediately in order to get to her 'schema-thoughts' appointment.

'Do you know what schema-thoughts are?' my father asks me.

'No,' I say.

I call the manager back and ask him to keep my mother there until I arrive. I drive across Edinburgh fast. When I arrive, the police have already taken my mother away to a normal emergency room, from where she is taken by ambulance to the psychiatric hospital.

My uncle, her brother, is already there when I arrive. I am eighteen and I have spent much of the past year going round to her house, sometimes finding the key deliberately kept in the lock on the inside for two or three weeks on end. I ring the bell and shout through the letterbox. I call her on the phone. She

234

never answers. I return and peer through the kitchen window at the back of the house, trying to work out if any of the dirty plates and pans have moved since the day before. I throw pebbles at her bedroom window on the second floor. I have no idea if she's alive or dead in here. When she finally opens the door to me, I have to step through dozens of empty bottles. Her sheets are sometimes soiled. She is usually filthy, in her bathrobe. One day she opens the door and I see a gash on the side of her head. She has fallen and hurt herself, although not badly. I know that she can be committed only if the police and doctors are convinced that she is a threat to herself or to others, so I always look for cigarette burns in the sheets as proof that she is about to cause a catastrophic fire, but I find few.

Her periods of isolation inside her house happen more times than I can count. I am studying to get into university, hopefully somewhere in the south of England, far away from Edinburgh. But I've planned another escape before that – a year off in the United States and France.

Paul and I greet each other in the hospital corridor.

'Hiya, Matt, how you doing?'

'Great,' I say.

'Yeah, me too. No fun this, is it?'

'Do you know what schema-thoughts are?' I ask him.

'No,' he says.

'Apparently Mum remembered she had an appointment to have schema-thoughts here. But I'm not sure.'

From a room off the cold, dark corridor, my mother appears in her slightly pilled beige coat. She is unsteady on her feet.

'Hi, Mum. How are you feeling?'

'Matty, I had to have my schema-thoughts,' she says immediately. 'A voice started to tell me to get to the hospital to have my schema-thoughts.'

She is trembling and she is sweet. She is not angry, not aggressive, does not try to hit me, as she has sometimes recently. For a very small woman with severe health problems, she is fiercely strong, and when she attacks me it is all I can do to hold her wrists, keep an eye out for her kicks and wait until she tires. But now she is lovely, vulnerable and in pieces. I feel enormously protective of her. Paul and I sense a rare opportunity, with both of us present and my being a little older than in previous crises, to persuade the doctors to take her in and make her better. We sit down with the doctor in his office. There's something about his manner – not overly concerned, it seems to me – that immediately makes me unhappy.

He writes in his notes that my mother, on admission,

> was beginning to shake – no other syms. of D-Ts [Delirium Tremens] other than above … Said she had been drinking too much recently and felt it was time to stop – otherwise there were no significant life events; she felt 'stupid and embarrassed' to be here … Speech appropriate thoughts – no formal thought disorder, no delusions, or hallucinations, nothing atypical other than behaviour described above. Mood – euthymic, denies suicidal intent, insight preserved.

We, of course, cannot see what he has written. Unless he looks more carefully at my mother's medical notes and enquires of us about her past, he will not understand what he's dealing with here.

His notes make a passing reference to a history of 'alcoholism and depression'.

'Ann is suffering from the effects of alcohol withdrawal,' he says. 'Delirium tremens. She just needs to dry out.'

'Yes,' I say, trying to remain calm but feeling the fury rising inside me and knowing that it shows on my face, 'but she's also mentally ill. She was talking about these "schema-thought" things, which obviously don't exist. She had a voice in her head telling her to come here. Do you get that from drinking too much?'

'Yes,' he says, 'it happens.'

The doctor says that there are only so many beds in the hospital and they are not really given to people who have drunk too much. Paul and I argue that my mother needs looking after.

'She may be suffering the effects of alcohol now,' I say, 'but she's otherwise very mentally ill.'

The doctor is impatient. 'You can't send her home,' I say. I am unwilling to compromise. Finally he agrees to have her stay the night.

The doctor writes in his notes that my mother 'refused admission for detox – despite encouragement from myself + family'.

On a morning in July, two months later, my mother goes to her doctor. She is showing severe symptoms of alcohol withdrawal again, obtaining diazepam to help her with the symptoms.

In October she turns up in another emergency room, in her nightdress and a sweater, smelling of stale urine. She has been found 'lying in road shaking … Claims that the BBC are trying to kill her by depriving her of cigarettes.' She says she has been told by her doctor that she would die of a disease named 'pledio-tony', clearly something she has made up. People are stealing from her, she says. She tells the doctor she is twenty-one years old. The doctor's diagnosis: 'paranoid psychosis + alcohol'.

'Her habit was to stay in bed with a bottle of sherry or whisky on the bedside table which she would drink until she fell asleep and drink more when she woke up until she fell asleep again,' he writes. 'She would only get up or leave the house in order to buy herself more bottles. Following this routine she would drink two or three bottles per day.'

On the day of my mother's admission, 3 October, I am packing my bags and getting ready to take a Greyhound bus the following morning. I have spent the summer living with my aunt and cousins in Newport, Rhode Island, and with my wages and tips have bought a pass that allows me to travel anywhere a Greyhound will take me. My first stop is New York. 'I am in the Museum of Modern Art in NYC,' I write in my diary. 'I'm now sitting in front of four Rothkos ... I'd like to stay here for hours.' I write about camping in North Carolina, cajun dancing in New Orleans, visiting the National Atomic Museum in Albuquerque, playing roulette and eating free pizza and drinking free beer in Las Vegas, gazing out across the Grand Canyon, getting lost for a few hours in the Rockies in Colorado. I read a lot: D. H. Lawrence when I'm in New Mexico, Jane Austen in North Carolina, John Steinbeck in Colorado, watching autumn turn to winter all across a continent I've never been to before this trip, a country that feels like a good place to be and an easy land in which to hide.

No one can call or write to me for nearly three months. There is only one mention of my mother in those pages of my diary, from 22 November, when I am in Vancouver: 'I phoned Jennifer. Mum is in a bad way. She was in hospital for some time, came out, got drunk, and is now back in.'

41

Again and again, as I read her medical notes – and some diary-like writings in her papers – I saw my mother entering the care of medical professionals and almost as soon slipping away.

'I am feeling very lonely and very sad,' she writes in July 1989, during a time when she apparently has a cancer scare and a test the following day. 'What have I done to deserve this – to lose so much that was lovely? I loved it, and I didn't want to lose it, for anyone's sake. Oh God – please let tomorrow be all right. I am frightened, and alone. I don't want the children to know.'

A few days later she writes: 'How oh how am I going to cope with all this boredom and loneliness? Christmas is a long time away.' In other words, when she would next see my sister and me.

Christmas 1989 was a catastrophe. I was home for the holidays from university in Brighton, and my mother was admitted to the psychiatric hospital shortly after I arrived. It was her seventh admission in just over a year, the notes say. And I saw, for the first time, a clear diagnosis from as far back as 1981: 'depressive illness … and then manic depressive psychosis'. But within the same paragraph she is described a few days after her admission as 'a well groomed, attractively dressed woman who was calm and composed, and able to give an articulate account of the difficulties of her life. Her mood was normal. There was no evidence of psychosis, she was cognitively intact.'

In those sentences, I realized, sat the constituent parts of the cocktail that destroyed my mother: an attractive, articulate, strong, well-spoken woman who wanted to cope and had an amazing ability to bounce back quickly from booze and madness; a woman who basically refused to get better by admitting she was ill and accepting long-term, not just stop-gap, treatment; and a medical team not willing or able to see how ill this woman was, how much she needed to be forced – legally if necessary – to take the pills that would make her normal, that would make her my mother again. The drinking was a veneer that they needed to see past and often failed to.

'I have now had the opportunity to review Ann's previous case notes,' a doctor at the hospital writes in 1994. 'There seems to have been the diagnosis of a bipolar affective disorder in the past, however hypomanic episodes have been somewhat clouded by her alcohol abuse.'

'It is quite difficult', writes her doctor in 1994 to the hospital, 'because of her past history of alcohol abuse and her personality to really be sure that she is suffering a severe degree of depression ...'

And then there was the painful possibility that all of this just took place a couple of decades too early; doctors now had more tools – better drugs, more social acceptance of mental illness – to help them treat people like my mother.

42

This is the entire contents of a letter postmarked 16 December 1990, and sent to me in Brighton:

Sat.
Matti – How to make 'Pommes Anna' for students.
Peel some potatoes – slice into thin rounds using Magimix.
Butter a pie-dish or similar. Put in potatoes (you could add chopped cooked ham or chicken in order to make a meal).
Cover with milk – add salt & pepper & grated nutmeg. (Use half [milk]/half cream if rich.) Cook in oven [at gas mark] 3 for 1 hour or more.
Try putting grated cheese on top – emmenthal best or if rich, gruyère.
VIP nutmeg essential.
xxx
M.

43

My mother's worst years began around 1995.

On 12 September 1995, she wrote from her home in Edinburgh to a doctor in Oxford.

'Thank-you for looking after me when I was in Oxford. I have come home, but I may go back. Could you please tell my husband that I love him, but I'm mortally hurt. Yours, Ann McAllester.'

And then nothing for five years. Not a single medical record. My mother all but disappears from my life during these years. I have hundreds of letters from her from this period, but they tell me nothing. They are manic scrawls of paranoia and delusion, written from hostels and bed-and-breakfast places in Oxford and Ireland.

She has sold her house in Edinburgh and has gone to Oxford to marry a priest, to enrol at the university, to uncover plots. Oxford is also the place where she can escape the sad memories of Edinburgh and be relatively close to Jane, who now lives in London. And then she goes to Ireland to bring an end to the region's conflict, to visit the places where she spent her child-hood summers, to uncover more plots. I have done my own bit of disappearing, having long since emigrated to the country where I felt at home when on the road after secondary school – the United States. I go to graduate school there, then become a newspaper reporter, hiding in Long Island's stories of murder and disaster and snipers.

If I'm in the States, I decide, my mother is not my

responsibility. There's nothing I can do for her. On 5 May 1994, I write in my diary of my family: 'It's like having someone die yet still seeing them around, unable to talk or touch or anything. My family is the walking dead.'

Some news of my mother does reach me. 'Mum sent that priest a box of rotten tomatoes,' I note in my diary on 24 October 1994, without further explanation.

I hear rumours that she may have been selling her body. She is without fixed abode now. At a youth hostel she befriends a young man who calls me when he is about to visit New York. I am like a stone on the phone because there's something about his tone that shrinks my stomach – not acknowledging that my mother is crazy, or perhaps he knows something about her he can use over me – and he doesn't call back.

I receive calls from landladies of two separate bed-and-breakfast places in Ireland.

'Your mother is drinking a lot and … you know,' the second one tells me. I'm touched that she has gone to the trouble of calling me in New York.

'I know,' I say. She's mad.

'I'm afraid she can't stay with me any more,' she says.

'I understand,' I say.

This lady is worried and kind, and I'm grateful my mother has found a forgiving hostess for a few days.

From a (bad) poem she wrote at the time:

> I wanted a home and children.
> What have I got?
> A single room in a lodging house.
>
> I needed company.
> I'm gregarious.
> What have I got?
> A lifetime of loneliness.

243

My sister and I talk of how our mother must be burning through her not-very-large savings. At times she believes she is the richest woman in the world. What will happen when she has nothing left?

I'm not quite sure how she has managed it, but my mother has made her way to the small city of Cork, in south-west Ireland, and has bought a small house. In early 1998, I fly in from New York to visit her.

When I arrive at the airport, I push my trolley out into the arrivals area and there are a handful of people waiting for the Ryanair flight from London. My mother has said she will pick me up, but she is not here. I have not seen her for a year. I look at the young parents and their two children, waiting for a grandparent, perhaps. There's the round old lady in the beige coat, unsteady on her feet; the greying middle-aged man; some others whose faces and bodies I scan. Oh, well, I'll dig out the address and get a cab, I think, a little worried about her not being here, because she had seemed so desperately excited at the thought of seeing me when we spoke on the phone. I push my trolley forward and the elderly lady in the tatty beige coat shouts, 'Matty!' and sways toward me, hurling her arms around my neck.

'Oh, Matty, Matty,' she says, very loudly, and starts crying and laughing. She holds my face in her hands with a scary strength and I smell her, picking up something of her sweetness underneath the wave of whisky and cigarette odour.

I lead her away from the people who are looking at us, and she sways and staggers. 'I did not recognize my own mother,' I think.

Her face is bloated, her big brown eyes sunk between puffed-up cheeks and a somehow heavier forehead. Her angles are all gone.

She looks a decade older and just very, very not like a normal person. She is ugly.

In the cab she barks her address at the driver as if he were a

244

semi-literate footman, and she begins to tell me in a loud voice how stupid the Irish are.

'They're the most ignorant people you have ever met,' she says. 'Plain bloody stupid.'

'Mum.'

'I'm sorry but it's true. They're the most ignorant bloody people you have ever met in your entire life.'

When the driver takes a left turn, my mother, sitting on the right of the passenger seat, flops heavily into the side of the car.

'I'm really sorry,' I say to the driver, amazed that he hasn't dropped us off before we've even left the airport. It seems the least he could do on behalf of the entire Irish nation.

'She was like this when I took her to the airport,' he says. Just my luck, he must be thinking, to have picked up this fare for the return journey.

At her house my mother has four pieces of furniture. In her room there is a mattress and a television. Both are on the floor. In another room there are two single beds, cheaply made but with clean sheets, ready for visitors.

'This is your and Janey's room,' she says, and it breaks my heart.

'Are you hungry, Matty?' she says, and sways towards the small fridge in the kitchen. 'I want to make you dinner. I had all sorts of plans.'

There is only a grimy frying pan in the sink and a few groceries – bacon, tomatoes, butter – in the fridge, and, besides, she can hardly stand.

'Why don't you go to bed and I'll make us a BLT,' I say. She goes to bed and lies on the mattress, propped up with pillows against the wall, smoking cigarettes and ranting. She picks on, in no particular order, my father, the government, the UN, the Germans and the Irish again. There is a dark-green plastic bucket next to her bed. Sometimes she has to take a pause from her angry monologue to cough and hack gobs of phlegm

245

into the bucket. This can go on for up to a minute. At other times she throws up into the bucket. And then she picks up her monologue where she left off. I'm not even looking at her much of the time. I stare out the window at clouds the colour of dirty sheets.

She has a coffee mug next to her, on the floor. I watch the football results come in on television and she drinks from her mug. I want her to be sober so that we can laugh, take a walk, cook a meal together, discuss my life in New York, gossip about my sister and my girlfriend. I want her to look after me a bit, perhaps, give me a bit of advice on a few things. I begin to look, quietly, for the bottle.

'What are you doing, Matthew?'

'Nothing,' I say, as I move the wastepaper bin next to her bed to one side. She knows what I'm doing.

'Sit down, Matthew.'

I lift her dirty bedclothes and hidden in the folds is a bottle of whisky.

'Don't be silly, Matthew,' she says.

'You have to stop drinking, Mum.'

'Give that to me.'

'No, I'm not going to. You're drunk. I came all this way and you're drunk. Couldn't you just stay sober for a bit, for my visit?'

She reaches for the bottle. She is small, but she has that improbable physical strength still.

'Don't be stupid, Matthew,' she shouts. 'Give that to me.'

We wrestle over the bottle, and I tear it away and walk to the other side of the room. She begins to cry. I remember the shock she has had in the past from stopping drinking too suddenly. The dangers of the DTs, delirium tremens. I am due to leave the next day. I will not see my mother before I leave. My real mother. Even if I keep the bottle and pour it down the sink, she will still be drunk or wiped out in the morning. If I keep it, she will just get up and go out, staggering, to buy more.

246

If I keep it, she will just shout at me. If I keep it and prevent her from getting more, she could have a fit and become delusional and even more of a danger to herself. So I give the bottle of whisky back to my mother, choosing to let her continue with her self-destruction.

She pours some into her mug, quietens down, and eventually falls asleep.

I go out and eat chicken and chips from the local chip shop. They are thick and heavy and give me none of the pleasure that they did, as the ultimate dinner treat, when I was a boy. I walk among the girls in their miniskirts and the boys with their hair kept in place with gel and wax. I have a pint in one bar, and a pint in another.

When I get back, my mother is asleep. In the morning she is still drunk and I hug her. She sobs desperately when I leave. But she can't get out of bed to see me out.

I've come to want a place even further away than America. In late 1998 the paper gives me a new job and I move to Jerusalem in January 1999, just in time to be pulled into the war in Kosovo, then the Second Intifada, then the days after 11 September, then Afghanistan, waiting for the Taliban a few miles away to fall, then Iraq to see Baghdad pounded by American bombs. It is an unusually bloody spell in history. It offers me as much war as I want, and I walk towards it every time with a huge sigh of relief: someone else's tragedy, something painful and frightening and pleasurable, something outsized and extreme, something both anaesthetizing and hypersensitizing, something more important than anything else. I cannot imagine living without it.

Swordle beach, Ardnamurchan

44

In early 2000, my mother asks my sister if she can come to stay with her for a week in London.

'As soon as I picked her up from Heathrow she announced that she had escaped, hadn't told anybody, but wasn't ever going back to Ireland!' my sister writes on 22 October, in a narrative composed for doctors who later treat my mother. My mother moves in with Jane – and stays. 'Within a few weeks she had started drinking and her behaviour became increasingly erratic,' my sister writes.

In the middle of August, our mother stops drinking suddenly, and the abrupt withdrawal brings on delusions. She believes a man has come to the front door and she is scared. She goes into the street in her underwear while my sister is in the bath. My sister leaps up, gets dressed and finds our mother in the nearby gym. Back home, she searches cupboards and under piles of bed linen for someone she calls 'the impersonator'. When my sister goes to work, our mother is in bed 'talking about someone called Simon who had asked her to marry him but was going to America, and seemed very sad that they would not have any time together', Jane recounts in her written narrative.

When my sister returns from work, the delusional behaviour continues and intensifies, and eventually she takes our mother to the A and E. Once there, our mother has several fits, gasping and foaming at the mouth. Ten days later, the hospital discharges her. Her behaviour worsens further and my sister reaches her breaking point. She calls social workers and doctors, and a group of about ten people – including police officers – come to her house and 'section' my mother, forcibly taking her to a locked psychiatric ward.

But amid all the awfulness is the start of something better. For the first time it feels as though she is going to get proper care and attention. The doctors' notes show a medical team in the local psychiatric hospital quickly piecing together a clear picture of my mother and her history and her illnesses. They do not mistake her for a drunk. Our mother has suddenly placed herself back in our orbit for the first time in many years, and we are no longer children. We are adults now, able to phone the social workers and doctors, able to impose ourselves on and understand bureaucracy. We are the only people our mother has.

I wake up at about six o'clock on 28 September 2000. Richard Poureshagh has arrived the night before from London for a week's holiday. 'Hey, do you want to see what I do for a living?' I ask him, and he jumps out of bed. We stand on my balcony and look across the valley to the Old City of Jerusalem, with the golden Dome of the Rock glinting in the first light of the day. We drive over, parking outside the Old City's walls, wending our way through the narrow alleyways until we get to the Western Wall. We're going to an event that no one thinks much of at the time. Israel's right-wing opposition leader Ariel Sharon has decided to make an early morning visit to the Temple Mount, as it is known to Jews (it is the Haram al Sharif to Muslims). Sharon is a figure of hatred for most Palestinians and Sharon is risking provoking their anger by stepping foot on one of Islam's holiest sites.

He is up and back in a matter of minutes and I'm busy getting a quote from someone when Richard taps me on the shoulder.

'Matt, I just heard some shooting,' he says.

What he has heard is the Israeli police firing rubber-coated bullets on the Temple Mount at Palestinians who have begun

251

to demonstrate against Sharon's visit to their holy place. A few Israeli soldiers rush down a walkway carrying an injured comrade on a stretcher, presumably the target of one of the many stones the demonstrators have begun to throw at the soldiers. The crack of the shooting is the sound of the Second Intifada beginning.

The war escalates and pulls me in completely. I want to be helping Jane, who has taken on the managing and the nursing of our mother, but this conflict is on my doorstep and all around me, and I can't abandon it. It is what I was sent to do by my newspaper and I can't help loving the work. For all the violence I am witnessing, I know that I have chosen the easy way. At the end of the day when I return to my flat in Jerusalem, I can close the door on the madness outside. But Jane has a madwoman living in her home for a year, except for the several times our mother is in hospital during that time, and it puts a terrible strain on her. Jane's loyalty to and need to look after my mother is absolute and unhesitating. I can stay away. I feel I have to, for my own sake. I am painfully aware of the unfairness to my sister in this.

My sister writes down a conversation she has with our mother on the morning of 22 October 2000:

Jane: What have you been up to this morning?
Mum: Nothing.
J: Writing letters?
M: One to Hungary.
J: What about?
M: Telling them to postpone [Uncle] Paul's trip as it's too dangerous while Milosevic is still around.
J: Do they ever reply to you?
M: No, sometimes I ask them things but they never write back.
J: Do you think they pay any attention?
M: Probably not.

J: And what capacity do you write them in?

M: As Empress and Tsarina.

J: Aah.

M: Don't you believe I am?

J: Well, I haven't seen any evidence of it.

M: No, neither have I. Maybe it's not right.

J: I don't think so.

M: It could all be a big waste of time. Maybe I should let them get on with it alone and get on with my own things.

J: Sounds like a good idea to me.

At the time, I am more caught up in the tragedies I am living amongst. Two days after my sister records the conversation with our mother, I write a piece for my newspaper about my neighbourhood, which spans Jewish West Jerusalem and Arab East Jerusalem. My next-door neighbour is an elderly man whose father sent him from Czechoslovakia shortly before the Second World War began. When he returned after the war, he told me as we sat in his living room, he discovered that not a single member of his family or any of his Jewish friends had survived the Nazis. So he returned to what was still Palestine.

'I often hear gunfire in the evening now,' I wrote.

Israeli men with guns and flak jackets walk around the Jewish part of the neighbourhood, keeping an eye on the houses. I'm not sure who they are or who pays them ... I went down to the Arab streets the other night to visit the family of one of the men who had died on the very first day of fighting, a middle-aged man who had gone to pray at the al-Aqsa mosque. He was shot in the head by Israeli police. The man's oldest son, Rifat, is twenty-two years old and since his father's death three weeks ago, he's been the head of the household. Rifat is an electrician and after ten days of the fighting, his Israeli employer told him that he was scared of Rifat and was thinking of firing him.

I am hiding, as usual, in the troubles of others. Among my mother's papers, many years later, I will find the following poem, written in 1979. It was a time when she was losing her sanity but often she was fine:

> My daughter is my child,
> Little dreamer of quiet dreams
> Flaring into flashing anger,
> Sucking a thwarted sulky thumb.
> My lover came and caused me
> To bear another me.
> But he left her
> A dimple,
> A sudden sparkle
> In the calm eye.
>
> My son is his father's child.
> I search in vain for
> For something I have given
> To my son.
> I watch his face in wonder.
> How can he have been
> So much a part of me
> Yet bears no imprint,
> No reflection?
> I gave him life.
> I give him love.

It is possible, I suppose, that my mother sensed early which of her children would be better at looking after her and which one would be more likely to run. Or perhaps she was just having a mad episode at the time of writing, because she never showed me anything but passionate love. Or perhaps both of my readings are accurate. However I read it the poem is not my favourite thing to read.

254

'Mum is very fragile, very dependent,' my sister writes in her journal on 19 January 2001. I am in Lebanon, writing about a massacre that took place there in 1982, and about Palestinian refugees.

> She is totally subdued and quiet, in constant need of reassuring and incapable of showing any interest in anything. Her [psychiatric] drug is to blame, it seems, I hope, and while the dose changes there does not seem to be any improvement. She dribbles and shakes, hardly talks and looks scared most of the time. When I am home she follows me round, often standing still as a statue behind me while I wash up or cook, wanting cuddles whenever I pause, even tapping me and asking for them sometimes. All I can do is take her gently in my arms, try and soothe her shakes away, feel how frail and bony she is, and tell her over and over that it is all going to be OK ... I just feel like bursting into tears half the time, and the slightest thing makes me retch – a funny smell or a new problem or issue to be tackled.

We use the money from the sale of our mother's house in Cork and some of my own savings to buy her a studio flat near my sister's place. I fly to London for several days and help move my mother in, reorganizing her furniture and possessions in the small flat. It's the least I can do. But I am soon off to Iran, another place so absorbing that I barely have time to think about my mother.

On 6 May 2001, she moves in to her new home. She is happy there but she still drinks, still has manic episodes, still has withdrawal seizures that require ambulances. She is a danger to herself.

My sister writes in her journal:

> On Thursday [7 June] I was off work [sick] and at about 6 p.m., Margaret, her upstairs neighbour, called me to say she was worried as Mum's door had been open all day, the key

was in the lock and she had called and poked her head in finding nobody at home. I went round and was worried to find all the lights on and her handbag sitting on the floor ... The next morning I went round on the way to work and found things as I'd left them.

My sister calls the police, who take the situation very seriously.

Filling the [missing persons] form in, popping home again to find a photo of her, brought it home that she is a very vulnerable person and I had absolutely no idea where she might be, that there were no friends to ask, no clues on where she might have headed off to. For the next couple of days I was sort of in limbo; was she dead in a ditch somewhere, still wandering the streets aimlessly and without money or shelter, or lying unidentified in some hospital?

Two days later, a nurse calls my sister from a hospital in north London. Our mother is there.

'Ann was admitted ... on 9th June after she was found laying [*sic*] unconscious outside a restaurant with a laceration on her head and feet,' a psychiatrist writes in my mother's medical notes. 'She went missing from her home on 7th June. Apparently she was drinking excessively and she had an epileptic fit.'

My sister drives to the hospital in Harrow and finds our mother in a ward next to the A and E.

She was very dazed and confused, still rather dirty and terribly small and sad looking ... Her feet were really cut and bruised from walking so much and in strange shoes that I didn't recognize and that hadn't fitted but other than that she seemed physically OK.

She stays in hospital for several weeks, convinced that she has been raped, demanding an HIV test. Then she returns

256

home. 'Ann believed that she can manage by herself and did not want to be sent to a residential home,' the doctor writes. 'Her daughter, Jane, believed that when Ann is discharged she needs support from Social Services.'

My mother attends art therapy and pottery classes. A community psychiatric nurse visits her. She has appointments with the consultant psychiatrist at the hospital. But she still lives alone, largely unsupervised, and she can still disappear at any moment into the endless streets of London. She can still be found on the street outside a restaurant, bleeding and unconscious. My sister and I yearn for something to be done, for some safe place to be found for her.

Later in the year she has another bout of drinking. In her drunkenness she fails to take her medication regularly and her mania returns. She is hospitalized.

As she gets better, in the locked ward, she has a realization that will change all of our lives. She begins to understand that she is bipolar, that she is not well, that if she continues to drink and not take her pills on time she will repeatedly end up in this sad, depressing ward. She tells my sister all this. More than thirty years after she first threw the Irish builders out of our house, she accepts that something is wrong with her.

My sister believes in my mother's commitment to not drinking, to taking her pills, and takes her on holiday to Crete in May 2002. In Crete, my mother is worried about what she considers Greece's readiness to lock people up for being mentally ill, and she makes Jane promise to be sure she takes her pills on time. At their first dinner, the waiter places a shot glass of local liquor in front of them both. My mother looks anxious, determined to stick to her abstinence but alarmed at appearing rude by declining the shot. My sister downs the firewater for her. And does the same every night. A couple of nights my mother takes a sip and giggles like a naughty child. She says how much she misses good wine. But she has turned a corner. In the future she will have the occasional drink, but never again will she drink herself into danger.

During the invasion of Iraq in March 2003, I am in Baghdad. A few days after the start of the war I am arrested and imprisoned by Saddam Hussein's secret police in Abu Ghraib prison, on the edge of the city. They suspect me, three photographers and a peace activist of being spies. 'This is going to devastate Mum,' I think, as I lie in my cell expecting to be executed at any moment. Rather against the odds, we are released after eight days, and when I return to London I expect to find my mother a complete wreck. She is so sanguine and calm about the whole thing that I'm mildly offended. 'You obviously did something very stupid to get locked up,' she tells me, after hugging me incredibly tightly and lighting a cigarette.

Later she says: 'You're not going back to that stupid place, are you, Matthew?' But within days I am back in Baghdad.

My mother's illness remains unpredictable. On 19 September 2003, about three weeks after I move to London to live there for the first time since my family left for Edinburgh when I was three, she is hospitalized again, and something has changed.

'She has not been sleeping well and has been agitated, pacing up and down and has been repeating that she has a brain tumour and things got worse over the last week as she became more mute, not responding and unable to function,' the doctor writes, recording what my sister tells him. 'When admitted, Ann was mute, not interacting, not socializing, very scatty in her speech, confused and there was a serious problem with her orientation, concentration and her memory,' the doctor writes. 'Ann's admission was quite different from previous ones.'

I have been spending up to six weeks at a time in Iraq. But when I am in London, I have time to spend visiting my mother in the locked ward and talking to her doctor. He and I sit in a visiting room before I see my mother.

'There is damage to the brain,' he says. She can remember little and she can't safely perform simple tasks like filling and turning on an electric kettle, he tells me. He draws a simple diagram on a piece of a paper. 'The white matter is damaged.'

He explains that white matter brings messages to grey matter in the nervous system. It can find new routes, new connections, but it is damaged, he says. It's the alcohol, the cigarettes, the hard living. They have run CT scans, blood tests and ECGs. The damage is irreparable. And then the doctor says something that I have wanted to hear for almost twenty years.

'I think Ann needs twenty-four-hour care,' he says.

'My sister and I agree,' I say, and somehow brain damage seems almost like a blessing. 'Thank you.'

When I'm taken in to see her, my mother is calm but lost. She spends month after month in the locked ward as Jane and I look, in partnership with social workers and the hospital, for somewhere she can live.

I am late for the cinema one Saturday afternoon because I have been visiting her. My mobile phone is dead and I have not been able to call, but Pernilla, whom I have only just met, has waited. There's no point in making an excuse. I tell her that my mother is very ill and explain that I was visiting her and so that's why I am late.

Some weeks later I am due to visit my mother. I haven't known Pernilla that long, but something makes me ask her. 'Would you like to meet my mum? You really don't have to. The hospital is not a nice place.'

'I'd love to meet your mum,' she says.

'Are you sure about this?' I ask. 'Trust me, it's grim in there.'

'Of course I want to come.'

We take the Tube up to the hospital and are buzzed in through the secure door. Pernilla sits in the visiting room, unfazed by the peeling paint, the reek of cigarette smoke and the insane people who open the door to see what's going on, and she falls into an enthusiastic discussion of ancient Etruscan art with my mother, who cannot make a cup of tea but remains perfectly capable of describing in detail the elongated sculpted figures of that period. I am pretty much left out of the conversation.

'She's so lovely,' Pernilla says, as we walk back to the Tube station after the visit. She has not patronized my mother, nor has she found her scary.

'That is a very nice girl,' my mother tells me when next I visit her.

I have a meeting with the doctor, and he tells me of a home they have found called Pine Tree Court. He warns me that it is a proper nursing home and that my mother, not yet sixty, may find the other occupants of the home to be depressing. I don't care. I want her out of the ward, which she shares with the crazed and the destitute, and so just about anywhere will seem an improvement. I visit Pine Tree Court with my sister and we agree that it will do. I pretend to myself that it doesn't smell of the dying and their final, insulting meals of boiled vegetables and grease.

My mother moves in and smokes in her room, against the regulations. The room has all the modern accessories of human collapse – the panic buttons and pull strings, the low toilet with supportive bars on the wall, the easy-wash carpets. It is a dulling, end-of-life motel room, stripped of warmth. A locked mental ward is a tough place, where some patients shamble along the corridor mumbling while others stride around with the certainty of their own angry brilliance, but it is not, at least, a place where you go to die. It is a place where you go to get better and then, in most cases, leave. No one at Pine Tree Court, we realize, has any plans to get better and leave. My sister takes my mother out of Pine Tree Court after a week and drives her back to the locked ward.

Every few days my sister takes our mother cigarettes and treats, and once a week she takes her home and cooks for her.

Sometimes I take her out for dinner. She drools and gets food on her face and moves slowly, attracting the attention of other diners and the staff. Sometimes I am embarrassed and ask her to wipe her mouth. My mother could not care less what anyone may think of her. She never has. That hasn't changed.

My sister has apparently limitless patience and strength. I can't spend too long with my mother without feeling completely drained and depressed. It is a failing of mine, I suppose.

'By the beginning of January there was a dramatic improvement in her cognitive function including her memory, concentration and orientation,' the doctor writes.

Jane and I have begun to notice the improvement too.

'I'm worried that she's getting too well,' I tell my sister.

'I know,' she says.

If my mother keeps getting better and advances into some zone of in-between wellness and illness, we fear that the doctors will reassess her, decide she does not need full-time supervision and cast her back into the world of the self-sufficient. Where she will, before long, open her front door and walk out again into London in her bare feet, forgetting who she is and where she is meant to be. And then my sister finds Rathmore House, a home for the aged. There's a room available on the top floor of this large house on one of the most beautiful, expensive streets in all of London, where famous writers and entertainers live and a small collection of shops caters to the wealthy. She has a room with skylights and windows and an en suite bathroom. A room with views of trees and gardens and pretty tiled rooftops. A room where she can have her own furniture and carpets and paintings on the walls, where she can smoke, where she can have an armchair for herself and one for visitors, chairs covered with throws and cushions in the rich tones of the Middle East. It's a short drive from the area where both my sister and I live. We get her a stereo and buy her CDs of classical music and old standards. She has books around and begins to read a few of them. Rathmore House is a short walk to a sweet little café, where for the first time in years she enjoys a bit of a social life, befriending other regular customers, who seem to find her eccentric but good company. There is a freak morning when an angry man murders one of my mother's and Pernilla's neighbours on the pavement with an axe. Other than that, it could not be a safer place to live. The staff look after her and dole out her medication. Doctors stop by. There is no pressure on her to socialize with the genuinely old people, and the staff seem to love having someone around who is a bit younger and feistier, a bit more independent. I visit, and Jane still takes her home for dinner once a week. (She asks me if I will cook for her and so I have her and Jane over one evening, but I am rushed and distracted and the food is mediocre and bland.) I sit in the second armchair in her room, and for the first time since I was a child we have calm, laughing conversations. I still edit myself a little (rarely do I mention my father), and I still have to bite my tongue now and then when she prods a tender spot. But for the most part, we are at peace. I take Pernilla round there. I take Rich there. My sister and I have as good a version of our mother back as we are ever likely to have. I had never considered an outcome like this to be even vaguely possible. Rathmore House is, at last, a place where my mother can be safe and happy. She moves in on 8 March 2004. She dies there on 6 May 2005.

That room in Rathmore House is my mother's due. Those fourteen months are her reward.

45

One of the rituals of death is the paid death notice in a newspaper. My sister had one placed in the *Scotsman*.

The letters began to arrive. My mother had alienated just about everyone she had ever been friends with and many people she was related to. As their letters arrived, I opened them and read them with uncontrollable shaking and tears. My sister received some also and passed them on to me. I could not begin to write letters of thanks to these people, many of whom I had not thought of for years. Some had known my mother since she was a child.

I put all the letters in a folder and for nearly three years I left them there, often thinking that I really should take them out and thank people for their kindness.

Now I felt I could open the folder. Nearly all of the letters were from people who had not seen or spoken to her in a very long time. The first letter brought instant tears, but now it was, at last, absolutely fine.

'For someone like me who saw little of her in her bad times, it is easy to think of her as she used to be – sparky, laughing, quite challenging but always full of enthusiasm and generosity,' wrote one old friend. 'And that is the picture I've retained over these long years.'

Another wrote: 'I got such a shock to read of your mother's death … We were at Kilgraston together and probably in the same hockey team together as well – she was always quite a laugh … I know she had been through some difficult times but I shall remember her in happier times.'

'Your Mum, on good form, was great company,' wrote another. 'We had some brilliant conversations on such topics as poetry, literature and religion. She was so intelligent and amusing. We used to have some very good laughs. The poetry class, which we both attended, was amazing. Her contributions were always intriguing and interesting. One constant in your mother's life was her devotion to you and Jane. I am sure you know that.'

'She was such a talented and fun lady when you were all little,' wrote the mother of an old friend of mine. 'That is the way I shall remember her. Illness is often cruel and was, I fear, in her case – may she rest in peace now.'

'Ann was such a lovely person,' an old friend wrote. 'I remember, with joy, the happy times we had with you all. On one particular occasion we were all going to a ball and I still remember how pretty Ann looked – her hair was in a short, sharp bob and she was wearing a straight, long black dress – she was stunning.' One very old friend says she is shattered by the news and acknowledges she might have done more: 'I feel I failed her – in fact all of us, her long-time friends, did.'

'She was my oldest friend,' another wrote, 'and I loved and admired her.'

A childhood friend of Jane's and mine, the daughter of friends of our parents during their time in London, wrote to my sister: 'You probably don't remember, but when we were kids we had an argument, you and Matt against Sophie and me – we were convinced that you were our cousins, you explained that we were not. We were so upset, because we loved your family – I think we were for ever smitten with the letter-shaped chips! ... I have clear impressions in the background of a pretty young woman with dark hair and lovely eyes, and the memories are all so affectionate.'

And finally, at the bottom of the pile, I found a letter from my father to my sister and me, written after my mother's funeral.

After I had given my eulogy at the funeral, I had returned to my pew to find my father crying.

'It's so true, so true,' he had said, meaning how my mother had taught us all to love. I grabbed his hand and kissed the side of his head.

A few days later he wrote to my sister and me.

I wanted to thank you both for everything you did to make the day of Mum's funeral so special. The whole experience was more important and meaningful to me than anything I had imagined. For me it truly felt as if the four of us were really together again for one last time and it felt so good. After the years of anger, bitterness and craziness it became difficult for me to remember all those enormously good times Mum and I had together. They got pushed so far away that I really had to work hard to conjure them up and sometimes even gave up trying. But standing there in the church with her so close to us I felt a wave of love and wonderful memories wash over me and finally after all these years it felt all right again. I hope that now she is with her God she might be able to feel the same way.

46

This is what I would have done were I reporting on my mother's medical care like a thousand stories I have reported in my time: I would have torn into the medical records and bureaucracy until I had what I felt sure was a definitive answer. I knew there were more records in the archives of the hospital in Edinburgh. Were I reporting my mother's treatment as I would the shooting of an Iraqi child or the whereabouts of Balkan war criminals, I would have milked the available witnesses – my father, uncle, aunts, friends – for everything they could remember. I would have offered the hospital the right to reply and they, almost certainly, would decline to comment. They would fear legal action, I imagine.

But I didn't have to report this story the way I always did. I could stop when I wanted to.

I did stop. And it felt right, deeply right. In trying to bring her back to me, I had never really intended to revisit my mother's darkest years. They had turned out to be inescapable and unavoidable. Her medical records had given me a chronology and a narrative of my mother's decline – and some explanation. It was enough. It turned out that I did not need someone to blame for it all. The fury I had felt, never clearly aimed in any one direction, had steadily subsided as I came to the end of her medical notes.

My mother's brain malfunctioned, that is all. People tried to make it work better and they failed and she slipped away. If the doctors made mistakes with my mother – and it's not as though I had found a smoking gun of negligence or malpractice – then they were just that: mistakes. No apology, settlement, investigation, or acknowledgment of error would keep my parents happy in their love, would turn my teenage years and my twenties into decades of warm family Christmases and holidays in Ardnamurchan, would give me a mother I could turn to about girls or school or work, would give me a mother who would look after me and cook with love for us all as she had before she fell apart, and nothing could bring her back.

Perhaps not even her cookery books.

47

Sunday, 27 January 2008, was a summer's day lifted up and transplanted into midwinter. I went for a run. The sky opened up in all its brightness over a London that had seemed suffocated for weeks by the withering grey of winter. I had been collecting some worries and wanted to pound them out. I was newly, if voluntarily, jobless. And in the coming days, Pernilla and I would try for the third time to create viable, strong embryos, to place them inside Pernilla, to make a baby. I was not sure how either of us could absorb the emptiness and silence that would come in the wake of a third failure. We did not discuss it. This time it had to work. But we were no longer making semi-joking assumptions about twins; we weren't stumbling upon nicknames for the embryos.

So I ran into the sunshine and, involuntarily, I thought about my mother. For some minutes I just wanted her, as I had so often since her death, to come back. I wanted her to look after me, to tell me that she would make everything all right. But for the first time this familiar desire began to irritate me in its pointlessness. It was a wish that was so divorced from reality that it was just a waste of time and energy. 'She's dead, OK?' I said to myself as I sped up along the pavement. 'And Dad will die. Understand that. No one will look after you as if you were a child. No one can do anything further to make this baby happen.'

And then I remembered again my mother's slightly stern face as she sat in her armchair in her room in Rathmore House.

She was rather pitiless as she began to speak the words I had thought about a thousand times since.

'If you need to keep the book open, you're not really cooking.' I was newly surprised by my memory of how severe she had looked as she said this. She was lecturing me, trying to teach me something important – even if she herself had, as my aunt insisted, never learned not to keep the book open herself. And I remembered a woman who had fallen apart for twenty years or more, and who had come back to us for just over a year, saying before she died that she was ready to go. She said she had cooked enough, gardened enough, read enough. Remembering those words stung a little, because she had also been saying, I realize now, that she had mothered enough. My sister and I were OK, she had decided. We did not need looking after any more. My mother had done her job. It had been imperfect, but that had not been her fault. She had given us, in our first years, enough to be getting on with for ever. She would be giving us no more. She was ready to go. She accepted her life, with all its hardships and disappointments, and she accepted its end.

In her state, she could never cook my meals for me again. She didn't even want to. Her battered mind, for all her recent stability, no longer allowed her to help much in sorting out the problems that her grown children faced, and she had known that, had tried to tell me that. I had to let go of that dream. Or so it seemed to me now. Of course, I had no idea if she had really intended her 'close the book' advice as a message beyond the kitchen. But that's what I decided she must have meant. I had to learn to cook for myself, to look after myself and to look after others. So she told me to learn to cook properly, so that I would not be reliant on the words and instructions of others, so that I could be in charge of feeding myself and other people on my own terms. Only when I could close my mother's cookery books, and close the book on my need for her, relying on what I had learned and on my own instincts and

269

my own creativity and my own willingness to take risks – only then could I move on with my life.

As I ran home in the gloaming, I decided that giving my mother's name to a daughter, if we ever had one, was actually a stupid idea.

The change had been happening for a while, without my noticing it much. In these months of cooking from my mother's cookery books, there had been some gradual changes. Less and less did I find myself drawn to the elaborate and the slow. I never got round to making anything from her Le Cordon Bleu file. I now wanted to cook simple and relatively quick dishes. OK, so perhaps that's because it's a lot easier to remember how to grill a piece of fish than to encase beef in choux pastry and then cook it at the right temperature for the right amount of time. But there was something more elemental, something more natural about my cooking. Cooking simple food made me understand and appreciate the ingredients more. I calmed down in the kitchen because there was less to worry about, and Pernilla came to enjoy being there with me rather than hating it – and the drill sergeant I used to become. I had toppled the regime of the shopping list, grabbing from the farmers' market or shop whatever looked good and then working out later what to do with it. It had all changed.

Here's an example. On a Friday in early January, I emailed my friend John, father of two small children, to see if there was any chance he and his wife, Kate, could come for dinner that night. I wasn't expecting them to say yes. As it turned out, however, they could. His parents were staying with them, so they had babysitters. I was delighted, but I had a lot of work to do that afternoon.

When John and Kate arrived just before seven, I was still at the supermarket. Some time after eight, I served dinner. There was a platter of jumbo shrimp briefly sautéed in olive oil, with garlic, fresh red chilli pepper, white wine, a little fino sherry because I ran out of white wine, and flat-leaf parsley. A

270

plate of serrano and chorizo. Red peppers sautéed with garlic until the peppers were droopy and melty and sweet. Beetroot boiled, peeled, chilled, and sliced into a salad with vinaigrette and whatever was at hand – spring onions, coriander seeds. Pernilla made perfect, garlicky hummus and, remembering a thousand lunches in the West Bank and Gaza, I toasted some pine nuts, diced some lamb, and fried the tiny morsels. I tipped out the pine nuts and lamb on to the hummus, scattered flat-leaf parsley on top, and drizzled it all with olive oil that a friend who lives in Israel had brought from the Golan Heights. There was pitta bread, close to what I would have had in the refugee camps of Nablus, warmed and delicious. And a salad of grated carrot, saturated in vinaigrette. And olives. And perhaps more. We drank fino and red wine and I found that I could cook without thinking much, and I could chat and laugh as I cooked, and I didn't find people in the kitchen an impossible stress, and the four of us ate and laughed with an ease that had never appeared when I had deliberated through the shopping and the chopping and the cooking, hoping to impress and shine. With that sense of freedom came something else, something just as useful if not exactly what I'd been hoping for. Cooking had not brought my mother back. It had been an amorphous idea in the first place, one that I talked myself into believing. I had tried to bluff my way past my own dogged atheism, my own immovable sense that when someone dies they really, truly are just gone.

I had convinced myself that through sheer will-power, through action, I could make something right that felt so wrong. I had hoped that I would find myself talking to her as I cooked, swimming in happy, food-sparked memories all the time. But while the process sparked off memories, there was no miracle. It had been a rather artificial and contrived plan, I now realized, the only thing I had been able to come up with in the first crippling blast of grief. The goal to memorize one hundred Elizabeth David recipes had faded away. It had increasingly rung false with me. I had continued to fill up my own recipe book, but more and more the recipes came from my own generation of cooks – Nigel Slater, Hugh Fearnley-Whittingstall, Jamie Oliver and others. Some I made up myself.

I continued to consult Elizabeth David, but I no longer felt obliged to her primacy in my kitchen. She remained a wonderful source of inspiration, but she was now one of many. Elizabeth David hated the way many in Britain treated her as a culinary deity while she was alive. It irritated the hell out of her. She might, frankly, have found my own period of slavishness somewhat distasteful. So, to some extent, I let her go. And with her, I had begun to let my mother go.

I would have considered that impossible for a very long time. A betrayal, in fact. But now it felt almost like a relief. She had been dead almost three years. It was time to stop struggling for the impossible. There were living people and hoped-for, not-yet-born people to look out for.

I went for another long run the night before we found out whether or not our third IVF had been successful. In the days after the implantation of the embryos and before the pregnancy test, I had slipped back into desperate yearning for it to work.

One evening, while we waited, Pernilla and I watched *Hannah and Her Sisters* on television. I had forgotten the ending of the film, when Woody Allen's character miraculously gets his new wife pregnant.

'I'm not sure if we can take another failed attempt,' I had told my father in recent days. 'I'm just not sure if I could cope with it.'

Running pounded out the swirl of panic and yearning. The rhythm of the minutes passing by as I ran through quiet suburban streets in Willesden clarified my thoughts and stripped away the pointless, restless wanting of things that were not within my control to bring about or to change. In the last three years I had ended what were, essentially, years of wandering and avoiding. I had come to London and made a home, and with Pernilla I had made my own family there. I had been blessed with just over a year of my mother's final happiness. And her death had given me a chance to rediscover who she had been before her illness struck her. I felt a new peacefulness as I came home in the near darkness. I might not completely pull it off, but I decided that, whatever the result of the test the next day, I would simply accept it. My mother's illness and loveliness and death had all finally taught me something.

Two years had not been too long – in fact, not long enough. But two years and nine months was finally sufficient.

We went out for dinner that night. I couldn't be bothered cooking.

⌘

Pernilla's Hummus

'This is tricky,' Pernilla said when I asked her for her hummus recipe, 'because I never use measurements, but here is my guesstimate:'

400–500 g chickpeas. You can use tinned or ones from a jar but dried chickpeas that have been soaked and cooked are so much better. (Soak them overnight in a bowl; change the water if you can remember or be bothered. The next day, put them in a pan and bring to the boil, simmering for half an hour to an hour and a half. Just keep trying them to see when they're done. Drain, but keep the liquid.)

Two big tablespoons of tahini.

The juice of one or two lemons, depending how lemony you feel like having it.

One big or two small cloves of garlic.

Approximately 100 millilitres of good quality extra-virgin olive oil; salt to taste.

Put all of the above in a food processor and blend until desired consistency – over a minute at least for creamy hummus, less if you want it more chunky, though I'd advise chopping up the garlic very finely in that case. Add more olive oil if it's too firm – or perhaps a very little of the chickpea liquid, if you used dried chickpeas. Or water. But even a little too much and it'll be sloppy and unpleasant.

Variations:

Adding a teaspoon of smoked paprika will give it a sweeter and more smoky flavour.

Adding some olive oil infused with hot chillies gives it a gorgeous spicy edge.

Adding a handful of roasted almonds gives it a rich, nutty texture.

My mother

Acknowledgements

I am indebted to Elizabeth David's two biographers, Artemis Cooper and Lisa Chaney, whose excellent, lovely books provided me with descriptions and biographical information that proved invaluable, especially in reconstructing the scene inside Elizabeth David Ltd.

My family and friends, many of whom appear in these pages, have been nothing but generous and patient, and they have my deepest thanks and love.

I will be grateful for ever to Flip Brophy for believing in this book from the second it popped, amorphous and raw, into my mind, and to the wonderful Sharon Skettini; to Beth Rashbaum for taking it on and giving it life and shape that I could not have found on my own; and to Susan Kamil for giving me one of the loveliest homes in American publishing, The Dial Press. In London, I was incredibly lucky to have Helen Garnons-Williams at Bloomsbury adopt the book and make it her own; and Erica Jarnes, who polished off the job with great patience. Felicity Rubinstein was an instant ally and helped me feel at home in my own town.

Felicity also helped me find what I had thought was a treasure lost for ever.

When I first met Felicity, my UK agent, she mentioned that her own mother had co-authored a cookery book in the early 1970s and that my mother had probably owned it. But because it was about cooking for the freezer, a sort of cooking that didn't interest me much, I rudely didn't even bother looking for the book. Weeks later, when searching through my mother's books for something else, I found on the shelves a paperback of the *Penguin Freezer Cookbook* by Helge Rubinstein and Sheila Bush. It now struck me as another connection and coincidence that, as with others before it, meant nothing and yet seemed rather powerful. I began to flip through the book and found my mother's handwriting on a recipe for koulibiac, a Russian salmon dish. My mother was, predictably, correcting the recipe a little. I flipped on and couldn't find any more annotations. And then the book fell open at page 144. There were stains on the yellowing pages. And, just back on page 143, the beginning of a recipe for strawberry ice cream. I had not been able to find my mother's strawberry ice cream recipe in Elizabeth David or any of the books I remembered my mother using regularly.

Written next to the recipe, in pencil, my mother had scribbled: 'V.G.'.

Very good.

I made it, and it was.

Please note: a few of the names in the book have been changed.

A NOTE ON THE AUTHOR

Matt McAllester is a Pulitzer Prize-winning journalist who worked as a reporter for *Newsday* for thirteen years, most of them as a foreign correspondent. He now lives in Brooklyn with his wife, Pernilla. Winner of a number of awards, including the Osborn Elliott Award for Excellence for his coverage of Nepal in 2006 and several Overseas Press Club citations for his international reporting, he is currently a contributing editor at *Details*.

A NOTE ON THE TYPE

The text of this book is set in Berling roman, a modern face designed by K. E. Forsberg between 1951 and 58. In spite of its youth it carries the characteristics of an old face. The serifs are inclined and blunt, and the g has a straight ear.